This Book Belongs To

For Zoe,
Happy Cooking!
Best Wishes,
Rose Grant

This book is for Gwen and all the great home cooks in my life; my grandmother Minta Ghering, my mom, Doris, and my mother-in-law, Jacqueline. Extra special thanks to B. J. Berti, and Jasmine Faustino at St. Martin's Press for all their help in making this book possible. Further thanks to Anne Wright for copyediting recipes and for making sure that all the i's were dotted and the t's were crossed.

Also by Rae Grant:

Crafting Fun: 101 Things to Make and Do with Kids

Copyright © 2008 by Rae Grant. All rights reserved. Printed in China.

For information, address St. Martin's Press, 175 Fifth Avenue, New York, N.Y. 10010.

www.stmartins.com

The written instructions, photographs, designs, patterns, and projects in this volume are intended for personal use of the reader and may be reproduced for that purpose only.

Written and designed by Rae Grant.

Compilation copyright © 2008 by Rae Grant.

Library of Congress Cataloging-in-Publication Data Available Upon Request

ISBN-13: 978-0-312-37779-3

ISBN-10: 0-312-37779-7

First Edition: October 2008

10 9 8 7 6 5 4 3 2 1

The creators of this cookbook have made every effort to emphasize safety precautions and safety procedures when children are cooking in the kitchen, and assume no responsibility for any child cooking without adult supervision. Any child in the kitchen should always be supervised by an adult.

Every effort has been made to obtain permission from publishers and copyright holders. Credit, when known, is listed as follows: Page 14, 17 19, 92, Magazine Cover 1923, Page 18, Julie C. Grant, Page 22, Sunkist New Day Drinks by Alice Brodley 1923, Page 28, 29, 32, 33, 34, Borden's Evaporated Milk Book of Recipes, The Borden Company. NY, undated, Pages 37, 88, 97, Dishes Children Love, by Culinary Arts Institute, Illustration by Beatrice Derwinski, 1954 Book Production Industries Inc., Page 36, 44, 90 The American Peoples Cookbook, Spencer Press, Inc., Page 66, Salads and Sandwiches, WWMC, Inc. 1927, Page 68, 70, 71, Planning, Planting, Preserving for Victory Gardens, the Ohio Fuel Gas Company 1945, Page 101, 108,113, 115, The Calumet Baking Book, 1931, Page 104, Pet Milk Cookbook, Pet Milk Company,1923, Page 128, 137, Best Chocolate and Cocoa Recipes Walter Baker and Company, undated, Page 134,135, Jell-O At Home Everywhere, 1922, Page 138, Knox Gelatine,1927, by Charles B. Knox Gelatine Co. Inc., Page 139 Frigidaire Recipes, 1928, Frigidaire Corporation

Cooking Fun

Fun

121
Simple Recipes
to Make
with Kids

Rae Grant

St. Martin's Griffin
New York

Table of Contents

Kitchen Memories

Many of the recipes in this book are old-fashioned and were family favorites at a time when food and treats were often homemade. Some of these recipes are very simple for new cooks to manage like Grandma's Cinnamon Toast (see page 28) and some require more help from adults like Yummy Turkey Meatballs (see page 86). Eventually, kids will find all of these recipes easy to make, but it takes practice and patience to get the best results.

Children often enjoy hearing memories about recipes and treats that have a relationship to family history. When I started to cook with my daughter, I began to tell her some of my favorite childhood memories and the relaxed times I spent in the kitchen making Snickerdoodles (see page 124) with my sisters. The kitchen was always a place where we could relax, talk, and have some independence as kids.

Family stories can have a magical quality to them. My grandmother was an exceptional home cook and baker. When we visited her house, the cookie jar was always full, and no matter how many we ate, more cookies magically appeared (or so we thought). She often told us stories about her childhood and how the farm hands came from miles around to have one of her mother's delicious country dinners. These types of memories are family treasures. A story and a recipe can quickly become part of one's family lore. There are pages in the back of the book (see page 140) for favorite recipes and notes. Kids can also start a collection of favorite recipes and stories using index cards or a notebook. However you go about it, have fun cooking with kids and creating new (and old) kitchen memories.

Rae Grant

www.cookingfunforkids.com

Introduction

Cooking and baking can be fun, rewarding, and delicious all at the same time. Making homemade food from scratch is a little like being a scientist, an artist, and a nutritionist. When you combine ingredients in just the right way, wonderful things happen. Cupcake batter will rise high to become a little cake, and a gooey egg will cook to be soft and creamy when you scramble it in butter. If you use too much salt or too little, you will certainly taste the difference! Learning to cook and bake is a great adventure, but it is also an acquired skill.

Working in the kitchen is a BIG responsibility. You are being allowed a new freedom in the family kitchen, doing things that are typically for adults. Be sure to take that responsibility seriously by following the rules of the kitchen. These rules will help you to succeed and keep you on track as you learn to cook and bake.

Even the greatest cooks in the world had to start at the beginning, just like you. Read through these rules and learn to put them into practice. Don't forget, adults are there to help, so don't hesitate to ask if you are unsure about anything.

Have fun learning to make these basic recipes, and visit **cookingfunforkids.com** for more *Cooking Fun* ideas.

Choices

When you learn how to prepare food, you will suddenly have a lot more choice in picking foods that you really like. Some kids like cooked vegetables more than fresh salads. Some kids prefer chicken to meatballs, and some would love a milk shake rather than rice pudding for a treat. You may even want to start helping with the shopping or making a list of food that you might like to have in the house and help plan and prepare a few family meals.

The choice is yours, and it would help out the adults too! Once you discover the wide variety of foods there are to choose from, you can begin to have a hand in making them. When that happens, a whole new world will open up to you.

Getting Started

Learning to be organized in the kitchen is part of becoming a successful cook. If you are organized and follow the directions carefully, your recipes will turn out successfully. Occasionally things will go wrong, but, generally, if you follow the recipes and directions, then you will have a creation that you can be proud of and, more importantly, that you will enjoy eating!

Kitchen Basics

• Always have an adult in the house when you are cooking or baking.

• Read each recipe carefully before you start. Be sure you have all the ingredients on hand.

• Tie back long hair or wear a scarf to keep hair out of your face and out of the food.

• Roll up your sleeves. This prevents them from getting in the way. If you like, put on an apron to keep your clothes clean.

• Prepare a work space on a counter or a table in the kitchen for your cooking project.

• Wash your hands with soap and warm water before you start handling food. When handling raw meat or chicken, or eggs, wash hands before and after with soap and very warm water. Wash any surfaces or utensils that were used when preparing raw foods with hot soapy water.

• Rinse fruits and vegetables before you begin preparation.

• Have all your ingredients out, measured, and prepared before you begin to cook. Always try to put ingredients away after you've measured everything. This helps to keep the counters clean and uncluttered.

• Don't hurry through the recipe. Take your time, and stay organized as you work. It's more fun this way and cuts down on what I call "kitchen distress" (eggs rolling off the counter or flour spilling on the floor).

• Clean up as you go. Have a bowl of warm soapy water ready in the sink. If you soak spoons and cups in advance, they will be much easier to clean later.

• Sweep the kitchen when you are finished. Leave it clean and orderly.

Safety Tips

Adult Help Needed • When you see this little icon, it tells you that you need adult supervision or help on a task.

• Use dry pot holders or oven mitts when handling ANYTHING that is hot. Oven mitts get old and worn out and heat can penetrate through damp material. Replace worn-out oven mitts and pot holders occasionally.

• Always ask an adult for help when using the oven or the stove.

• Never leave the kitchen when the stove or oven is in use. Stay near the food while it is cooking.

• Turn the handles of the pans and skillets in towards the middle of the stove top and away from any heat source. This will also help avoid burning and spilling accidents.

• Let pots and pans cool before putting them in the sink.

- Never leave sharp knives or any sharp object in the sink or on the counter.

- Clean knives properly, and wipe them dry carefully by always keeping the sharp edge of the blade down. Have an adult help you put them away.

- Ask an adult if there is a serrated knife in the kitchen that you can use. It's a good knife for beginners to use.

- When using sharp knives, ask an adult to show you the proper way to use it.

- Always cut foods on a plastic or wooden cutting board, and not on the counter surface.

- Graters can skin fingers. Hold the grater with one hand and grate the food in the front of the grater. Keep fingers on the outside, away from the holes.

- Never touch any electrical appliance with wet hands or place any electrical appliance in or near water. You could get a shock or worse.

- Blender blades are very sharp. Ask an adult for help when assembling, disassembling, and cleaning the blender blade.

Equipment

Box grater
Blender
Can opener
Colander
Cutting board
Electric mixer
Juicer
Kitchen timer
Knives
  8-inch serrated knife
  8-inch chef knife
  small paring knife
Ladle
Measuring cups (for liquid)
Measuring cups (for dry ingredients)
Measuring spoons
Mixer
Mixing bowls
Mixing spoons
Oven mitts and pot holders
Pastry brush
Pots and pans
  baking pan (8- and 9-inch)
  baking sheet
  saucepans with lids
  skillet (7-, 8-, and 9–inch)
  loaf pan
  muffin pans
  pot with lid (8-quart)

Potato masher
Rubber spatula
Rotary beater
Saucepans with lids
Spatula (for turning food)
Strainer
Tongs
Vegetable brush
Vegetable peeler
Wire whisk
Wire rack
Wooden spoons (long- and short-handled)

Baking and Cooking Extras:
Aluminum foil
Double boiler
Kitchen towels
Paper muffin-tin liners
Parchment paper
Waxed paper
Waxed paper bags
Wooden toothpicks

Green Kitchens

Reduce plastic by using waxed paper, a clean dish towel, or clean plate when covering a bowl for food that needs refrigeration.

Use waxed paper and waxed paper bags to wrap lunch food.

Reuse plastic containers and lids as many times as possible before recycling in the trash.

Reuse plastic bags by cleaning and drying them. After rinsing, place a small magnet on the inside of the bag and attach it to the side of the refrigerator to dry.

Use canvas bags when shopping. It may take a few weeks to train you and your family, but eventually you will reduce the number of plastic bags you use.

Recycle Read about what types of items your town or city recycles, and throw away accordingly.

Talk about recycling at school and at home to figure out the simple things you can do to help cut down on wasting resources locally.

Start a green club with your friends, and research the issues and solutions that surround recycling.

10

Cooking Terms

Bake to cook food in a hot oven

Beat to stir quickly and repeatedly until a mixture of flour and liquid is combined

Blend to mix foods together thoroughly with a wooden spoon, electric mixer or wire whisk

Boil to cook liquid until it bubbles and breaks the surface

Bread to coat food with eggs, flour, bread crumbs or Parmesan cheese

Broil to cook food directly under a heat source such as a toaster oven

Chill to cool an ingredient in the refrigerator until it is cold

Chop to cut food into smaller pieces with a sharp knife

Coat to cover an ingredient with a thin outer layer, such as flour, sugar, or spices

Combine to stir two or more ingredients together until they are mixed well and do not separate

Cool to let a food stand at room temperature until it is no longer warm

Cream to mix 1 or more foods (usually butter and sugar) with a spoon or an electric mixer until soft and creamy

Fold to combine a lighter ingredient with another heavier ingredient by gently cutting down through the mixture with a spatula or spoon and sliding it across the bottom of the bowl and up the other side.

Frost to cover or decorate a cake or cookie with frosting or icing

Fry to cook food, such as an egg, in a small amount of hot oil or butter over moderate to high heat,

Garnish an edible decoration added to finished dish, such as mint leaves

Grate to shred foods into smaller piec by rubbing against a box grater

Grease to rub the surface of a pan or dish with butter or oil to prevent food from sticking.

Mince to finely chop or cut food into very small pieces

Mix to combine 2 or more ingredients by stirring with a spoon or using an electric mixer

Pan fry (sauté) to cook food in a ski over high heat in a small amount of oil or butter

Peel to strip off the outer covering or skin of fruit and vegetables, such as potatoes, carrots, oranges, or bananas

Poach to cook food gently in simmeri (not boiling) liquid

Puree to grind food until it is completely smooth, such as broccoli

Simmer to cook over low heat as small bubbles break the surface

Steam to cook food in a pot with a steam basket until it is soft

Stir to mix with a spoon in a circular or rotating motion

Toss to gently mix ingredients togethe by turning them over using two forks o a fork and a spoon

Whisk to beat quickly ingredients with fork, wire whisk, or mixer until they ar light and fluffy

Zest the outside skin of citrus fruit which you rub on the fine holes of a bo grater or small grater

How to Measure

To measure dry ingredients, use graduated measuring cups: (¼ cup, ⅓ cup, ½ cup and 1 cup) or graduated measuring spoons (¼ teaspoon, ½ teaspoon, 1 teaspoon, 1 tablespoon).

Use graduated cups and spoons to measure flour, sugar, bread crumbs, cornmeal, oatmeal, and other types of dry ingredients such as cocoa powder, baking soda, and salt. You can also use graduated measuring cups and teaspoons to measure peanut butter, oil, and butter.

To measure flour or granulated sugar, lightly spoon the flour into a cup. Use the straight edge of a butter knife to level off.

To measure brown sugar, spoon the brown sugar into the cup and press down with the back of a teaspoon. Pack until it holds its shape when the cup is turned upside down.

Measure baking powder and baking soda exactly. Fill a measuring spoon heaping full and use the straight edge of a butter knife to level off. Too much or too little may produce poor results with quick breads and cakes.

To measure melted butter, first melt the butter, then measure by level tablespoons.

To measuring sticky liquids or syrups such as molasses, honey, or maple syrup, pour the liquid into a measuring cup or measuring spoon. Don't dip the spoon in the jar. Too much of the liquid will cling to the spoon, making it hard to measure.

To measure liquids such as milk, water, juice, and oil use liquid measuring cups. These come with 1 cup, 2 cup, 4 cup, and 8 cup measurements. For smaller amounts use a graduated measuring spoon.

Use a ruler to measure a roasting or baking pan. Measure from the top inside for length, and width. To measure the depth of the pan, place the ruler on the inside base and measure the side from the bottom to the top.

Use the measuring chart to the right or on the inside cover of this book as a quick reference guide.

Measuring Equivalents

dash = less than ⅛ teaspoon

3 teaspoons = 1 tablespoon

4 tablespoons = ¼ cup

5 tablespoons + 1 teaspoon = ⅓ cup

8 tablespoons = ½ cup

11 tablespoons = ⅔ cup

12 tablespoons = ¾ cup

16 tablespoons = 1 cup

1 cup = 8 fluid ounces

1 cup = ½ pint

2 cups = 1 pint

4 cups = 1 quart

4 quarts = 1 gallon

16 ounces = 1 pound

12 ounces = ¾ pound

8 ounces = ½ pound

4 ounces = ¼ pound

11

Beverages

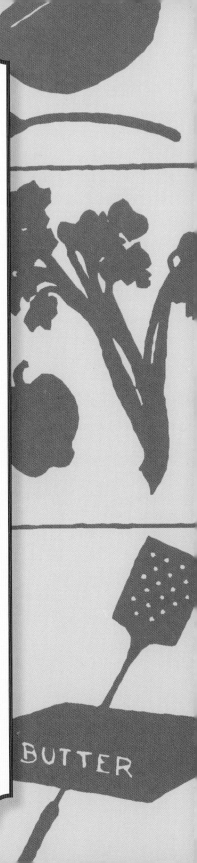

Hot Cocoa

✦

Can't Sleep Hot Milk and Honey

✦

Wake-Up Breakfast Drink

✦

Banana Breakfast Shake

✦

Gwen's Fruit Smoothie

✦

Blueberry Smoothie

✦

Honey Orange Spritzer

✦

Lemon Fizz

✦

Lemonade by the Glass

✦

Sugar Syrup

✦

Pitcher of Lemon-Limeade

✦

Grape Juice Refresher

✦

Chocolate Sauce

✦

Chocolate Milk

✦

Vanilla Shake

✦

Egg Cream

BUTTER

Hot Cocoa

Classic hot cocoa is easy to make. Add a teaspoon of homemade whipped cream (see page 139) to the cup before filling with hot cocoa.

1 cup milk

1 tablespoon sugar

2 teaspoons unsweetened cocoa powder

Adult Help Needed

1. Pour the milk into a small saucepan. Add the sugar and cocoa to the milk, and turn heat on medium-low. (The sugar and lumpy cocoa will begin to melt in the warm milk.) Use a small whisk to stir the mixture until well blended. Whisk for about 4 minutes, until the milk is hot but not boiling. (Whisking will make the cocoa frothy and smooth.)

2. Using a pot holder, remove pan from the heat. Pour hot cocoa into a cup and serve with hot buttered toast.

Serves 1

Can't Sleep Hot Milk and Honey

Try this relaxing drink before bedtime, especially if you are having trouble going to sleep.

1 cup milk

1 teaspoon honey

¼ teaspoon vanilla extract

Pinch of nutmeg

Adult Help Needed

1. Pour the milk into a small saucepan. Add the honey and vanilla to the milk, and turn heat on medium-low. (The honey will begin to melt in the warm milk.) Use a small whisk to stir the mixture until well blended. Whisk for about 4 minutes, until the milk is hot but not boiling.

2. Using a pot holder, remove pan from the heat. Pour the milk into a cup. Sprinkle a little nutmeg over the frothy top. Sweet dreams!

Serves 1

Wake-Up Breakfast Drink

Not only for mornings, you can also serve this light and frothy orange juice and milk drink for a quick pick-me-up after school.

½ cup cold orange juice

½ cup cold milk

¼ teaspoon vanilla extract

Adult Help Needed

Put the orange juice, milk, and vanilla in a blender. Cover with the lid. Turn on the blender to high speed and blend until smooth and frothy. Pour the drink into a tall glass. Serve right away.

Serves 1

Banana Breakfast Shake

If you have extra bananas on hand, try it in this creamy shake.

1 banana, peeled

¾ cup cold milk

4 to 6 ice cubes

Adult Help Needed

Put the banana, milk, and ice cubes in a blender. Cover with the lid. Turn on the blender to high speed and blend until smooth and frothy. Pour the shake into a tall glass. Serve right away.

16

Serves 1

Gwen's Fruit Smoothie

My daughter, Gwen, perfected this recipe as her first blender concoction. For a more intense sweet-tart flavor, try adding raspberries.

1 cup fresh or frozen strawberries

1 banana, peeled

½ cup orange juice

4 ice cubes

1. If you are using fresh strawberries, rinse them and remove the green cap from the tops. Put the berries, banana, orange juice, and ice cubes in a blender. Cover with the lid. Turn on the blender to high speed and blend until smooth.

Adult Help Needed

2. Pour the smoothie into a tall glass or 2 small glasses and serve right away.

Serves 1 or 2

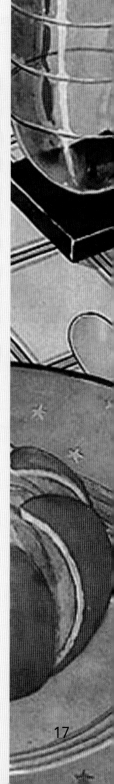

Blueberry Smoothie

Blueberries are nutritious and delicious. Make this drink anytime you want something smooth, sweet, and refreshing.

1 cup fresh or frozen blueberries

½ cup plain yogurt

½ cup milk

2 tablespoons honey

1 teaspoon lemon juice

Adult Help Needed

1. Put the blueberries, yogurt, milk, honey, and lemon juice in a blender. Cover with the lid. Turn on the blender to high speed and blend until smooth.

2. Pour the smoothie into 2 glasses and serve right away.

Serves 1 or 2

Add-Ins

Use ½ cup chopped fresh mango with the blueberries.

For a sweeter, thicker texture, add 1 peeled banana.

Honey Orange Spritzer

It's fun to make your own soda drinks. Experiment with various combinations of juices to find which flavors you like best.

¼ cup orange juice

1 teaspoon honey, or more to taste

Seltzer, chilled

Combine the orange juice, honey, and chilled seltzer in a tall glass. Add the ice cubes. Stir and sweeten with more honey or orange juice to taste. Serve right away.

Serves 1

Lemon Fizz

Seltzer, chilled

2 tablespoon fresh lemon juice

1 teaspoon confectioners' sugar

Fill a tall glass half full with chilled seltzer. Add the lemon juice to the seltzer. Stir in the confectioners' sugar while the seltzer is bubbling. Test for sweetness. Serve right away.

Serves 1

19

Lemonade by the Glass

Everybody loves lemonade. It's a great drink on a hot summer day. Here's a basic recipe you can use to make a glass of homemade lemonade.

3 tablespoons Sugar Syrup (recipe below)

1 to 2 tablespoons fresh lemon juice

1 cup cold water

In a tall glass mix together the Sugar Syrup, lemon juice, and water. Add ice cubes and enjoy.

Serves 1

Sugar Syrup

1 cup sugar

1 cup water

Adult Help Needed

1. In a medium saucepan combine the sugar and water. Turn heat on over medium-low and cook, stirring until the sugar is dissolved.

2. Using a pot holder, remove pan from the heat. Cool the syrup to room temperature, then pour in a jar and refrigerate, covered, until ready to use. (The syrup will keep for weeks in the refrigerator.)

Makes 6 to 8 servings

Pitcher of Lemon-Limeade

For a new twist on lemonade, try adding lime juice to the mixture.

¾ cup fresh lime juice (about 6 limes)

¾ cup fresh lemon juice (about 4 lemons)

1 recipe Sugar Syrup (see page 20)

4 cups cold water

Lemon and lime slices or fresh mint leaves for garnish

1. Slice the limes and lemons in half. Use a small hand juicer to squeeze the juice. You should have about ¾ cup each of lime juice and lemon juice. Pour juices into a large pitcher.

2. Stir in the Sugar Syrup and water. Add ice cubes. Garnish with lemon and lime slices or fresh mint leaves.

Serves 6 to 8

Grape Juice Refresher

This drink is similar to an old-fashioned party punch.
Make it for any special occasion.

¼ cup grape juice

¼ cup orange juice

Ginger ale, chilled

Lemon slices and fresh mint for garnish

Combine the grape juice, orange juice, and chilled ginger ale in a tall glass. Add ice cubes and stir. Garnish with a slice of lemon and a sprig of mint. Serve right away.

Serves 1

Chocolate Sauce

*Use chocolate sauce to make chocolate milk and shakes.
This will keep for weeks when refrigerated.*

1 cup sugar

1 cup unsweetened cocoa powder

1 cup water

1 teaspoon vanilla extract

Adult Help Needed

Combine the sugar, cocoa, and water in a medium saucepan. Turn heat on low and cook the sauce for 4 minutes or until thick. Whisk occasionally to smooth out lumps. Let cool, then add the vanilla. Stir well. Store in a glass jar with lid and refrigerate.

Makes about 1 cup

Chocolate Milk

Chocolate milk is always good as an after-school treat, especially when you use homemade chocolate sauce.

1 cup cold milk

1 tablespoon Chocolate Sauce (recipe above)

Combine the milk, and Chocolate Sauce in a tall glass. Stir briskly until chocolate is blended in the milk. Serve right away.

Serves 1

Vanilla Shake

A long time ago, shakes were made with milk and a flavored syrup shaken in a jar. Once ice cream became widely available, it was added to the mix for a thick and creamy result.

2 cups good quality vanilla ice cream

½ cup milk

Adult Help Needed Put the ice cream and milk in a blender. Cover with lid. Turn on the blender to high speed and blend until smooth. Pour into a tall glass and serve right away with a spoon or a straw.

Serves 2 or 3

Add-Ins

Chocolate Shake: Combine ¼ cup of Chocolate Sauce to the Vanilla Shake. Turn on the blender to high speed and blend until smooth.

Strawberry Shake: Combine 1 cup fresh or frozen strawberries with the Vanilla Shake. Turn on the blender to high speed and blend until smooth.

Egg Cream

Egg creams are a frothy chocolate milk beverage that contain neither egg nor cream. Years ago, this drink became famous in New York City soda fountains, but it is very simple to make at home.

3 tablespoons Chocolate Sauce (see page 23)

¼ cup cold whole milk

1 cup seltzer, chilled

1. Chill a tall glass in the freezer for 2 to 3 minutes. Pour the Chocolate Sauce in the bottom of a tall chilled glass. (***Don't stir yet.*** Add the milk. You will have a layer of chocolate and a layer of milk in the bottom of the glass.

2. Pour the cold seltzer in the glass and stir vigorously with a long spoon until foamy. Serve right away.

Serves 1

Toasts, Sandwiches, and Soups

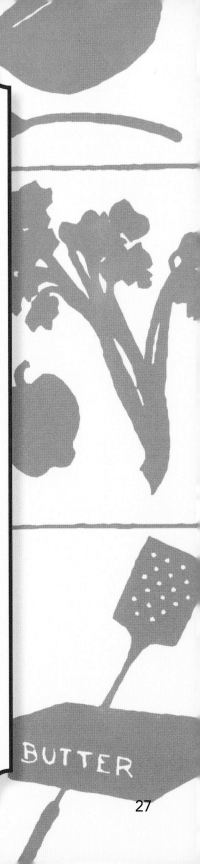

Grandma's Cinnamon Toast

Toast and Spreads

French Toast and Toppings

Avocado Toast and Guacamole

Cheese Toast

Grilled Cheese and Tomato

Croque Monsieur

Turkey BLT

Tuna Salad

Blueberry Soup

Chicken and Rice Soup

Old-Fashioned Potato Soup

Easy Cheesy Broccoli Soup

Emergency Soup

Creamy Tomato Soup

BUTTER

Grandma's Cinnamon Toast

When we visit Grandma's house in the winter, she makes this sweet, buttery toast every morning for the kids. Serve with steaming Hot Cocoa (see page 14) for a perfect cold-weather treat.

4 teaspoons sugar

¼ teaspoon ground cinnamon

2 slices bread

1 tablespoon butter, softened

1. In a small bowl mix the sugar and cinnamon. Set aside.

2. Toast the bread slices until golden brown. Spread the toast with butter while hot. Sprinkle the Cinnamon-Sugar on the toast so that it melts into the butter to make a thick layer. Cut the toast diagonally in half to make triangles. Eat right away.

Serves 1 or 2

Cinnamon-Sugar

Mix up a jar of Cinnamon-Sugar that will last for months.

In a small bowl mix 1 cup sugar and 2 tablespoons ground cinnamon. Store in a pretty glass jar with lid or a decorative shaker.
Makes 1 cup

Toasts and Spreads

Toast may seem ordinary, but it can be transformed into any number of dishes. Try these suggestions for breakfast or an after-school snack. Experiment with different types of bread, and be sure to make a list of your favorite combinations.

Cinnamon raisin bread, peanut butter, apple slices

Pumpernickel bread, cream cheese, chopped chives

Multigrain bread, hummus, cucumber slices

Corn bread, strawberry slices

Wheat bread, avocado slices, sliced Cheddar cheese

Sourdough bread, olive oil, chopped tomato

Banana bread, cream cheese, dried cranberries

Brioche or challah, sliced bananas, chocolate sauce

French Toast

French Toast is an old-fashioned way to use day-old bread. In our home, we serve it for breakfast, and we sometimes have it for a midweek supper. If your bread is extra dry, add a little more milk or water to the egg mixture and let the bread soak until moist.

1 egg

2 tablespoons milk

2 slices bread

1 tablespoon butter

Maple syrup to taste

1. In a shallow bowl wide enough to hold 1 slice of bread flat, combine the egg and milk. Whisk with a fork until well blended.

2. Dip 1 slice into the egg mixture until it is completely moistened. Place the soaked bread on a plate. Moisten the second slice in the same way and place it on the plate.

Adult Help Needed

3. In a skillet that will hold both slices of bread, melt the butter over medium-low heat. Using a pot holder, tilt the skillet so the butter spreads evenly around the bottom of the pan.

4. Place the soaked slices in the hot skillet. After 3 minutes, use a spatula to lift up the slice and check that it is nicely browned underneath. When it is browned, flip it and fry the other side until golden brown. Place the slices on clean plates. Serve with maple syrup.

Serves 1 or 2

Toppings

In place of maple syrup (or along with it), top French Toast with fresh fruit such as blueberries, sliced strawberries, bananas, or peaches. Dust with confectioners' sugar.

Jam Syrup

Place 3 tablespoons of your favorite jam and 1 teaspoon water in a small saucepan. Warm over medium-low heat until jam is melted. Pour warm sauce over French Toast. *Serves 1 or 2*

Honey Butter Sauce

Heat ¼ cup butter and 2 tablespoon honey in a small saucepan. Warm over medium-low heat, stirring until smooth. Serve warm over French Toast. *Serves 3 or 4*

Honey Orange Butter

Place ¼ cup softened butter, 1 teaspoon of zested orange peel, and 2 tablespoon honey in a small bowl and stir until well blended and smooth. Spread generously over hot French Toast. *Serves 4*

Avocado Toast

A perfectly ripe avocado spread on toasted bread is delicious any time.

1 ripe avocado

1 teaspoon fresh lemon or lime juice

¼ teaspoon salt

Pinch of freshly ground pepper

2 slices whole wheat bread

Adult Help Needed

Cut the avocado in half using a paring or serrated knife. Use a spoon to remove the pit, then scoop out the pulp. Place the pulp in small bowl and mash lightly with a fork. Add the lemon or lime juice, salt, and cayenne pepper to taste. Toast the bread in the toaster until golden. Spread the avocado mixture on toasted bread. Eat right away.

Serves 2

Guacamole

In a small bowl mash 1 ripe avocado with a fork. Add ½ cup chopped tomato, ¼ cup chopped onion, 1 tablespoon chopped cilantro, juice of 1 lime, and a big pinch of chili powder to the mixture. Add salt to taste. Stir lightly with a fork to combine. Serve with tortilla chips or spread on toast. Eat right away.

Cheese Toast

Cheese toast is good for breakfast, lunch, or a light supper. Try some of the Add-Ins listed at the end of the recipe to find your favorites.

2 slices Cheddar or Swiss cheese

2 slices whole grain bread

Adult Help Needed

Place the cheese on the bread. Place in toaster oven and toast until cheese is golden and bubbling, about 3 to 4 minutes. (Stay with your toast; it can burn easily.) Serve right away.

Serves 1 or 2

Add-Ins

Before adding the cheese, place one or more of the following on each slice of bread:

1 slice tomato

1 to 2 thin slices of red onion

3 slices apple or pear

½ cup Tuna Salad (see page 37)

Grilled Cheese and Tomato

The secret to making the perfect grilled cheese is spreading a generous amount of butter on the outside of the sandwich before you grill it. This allows a golden crust to form. Feel free to experiment with different cheeses.

1 tablespoon butter, softened

2 slices sandwich bread

2 to 3 slices Cheddar cheese

1 slice tomato

Adult Help Needed

1. Spread the butter on one side of each bread slice. Place one slice of bread, buttered side down, on a plate or a cutting board. Top the unbuttered side with cheese and tomato. Place second slice on top, making sure the buttered side is up.

2. Heat a small skillet over medium-low heat. When the skillet is hot, place the sandwich in the pan. Cook until the underside is golden brown, about 4 minutes, gently pressing the sandwich flat as it grills. (Pressing helps the cheese to melt faster.) Use a spatula to flip the sandwich over. Grill the other side to the same golden brown.

3. Place the sandwich on a serving plate. Cut it in half and serve hot. Serve with Creamy Tomato Soup (see page 44) and Carrot Curls (see page 69).

Serves 1

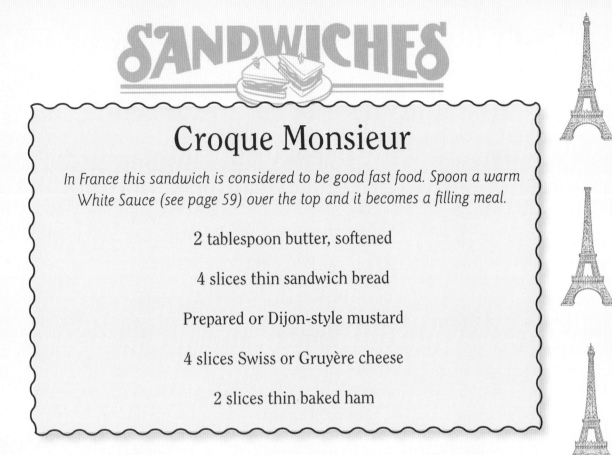

Croque Monsieur

In France this sandwich is considered to be good fast food. Spoon a warm White Sauce (see page 59) over the top and it becomes a filling meal.

2 tablespoon butter, softened

4 slices thin sandwich bread

Prepared or Dijon-style mustard

4 slices Swiss or Gruyère cheese

2 slices thin baked ham

Adult Help Needed

1. Spread the butter on one side of each bread slice. Place one slice of bread, buttered side down, on a plate or a cutting board. Lightly brush the unbuttered side of 1 bread slice with mustard, then top with cheese and ham. Place second slice on top, making sure the buttered side is up.

2. Heat a small skillet over medium-low heat. When the skillet is hot, place the sandwich in the pan. Cook until underside is golden, about 4 minutes, gently pressing the sandwich flat as it grills. (Pressing helps the cheese to melt faster.) Use a spatula to flip the sandwich over. Grill the other side to the same golden brown.

3. Place the sandwich on a serving plate. Cut in half and serve hot. You may want to eat this with a knife and fork.

Serves 2

Turkey BLT

A BLT gets even better when you add a few slices of turkey. Serve with a Lemon Fizz (see page 19) and you'll have a meal worth staying home for!

4 slices bacon

4 slices multigrain bread

2 teaspoon mayonnaise

4 slices turkey

2 large crisp lettuce leaves

2 thin tomato slices

Adult Help Needed

1. Line a plate with 2 paper towels. Place the bacon slices in a medium skillet. Turn on heat to medium-low and cook until almost crisp, about 4 minutes. Using a fork, turn the slices over and cook until golden brown, about 4 minutes longer. Place cooked bacon on paper towels to drain.

2. Toast the bread. For each sandwich, spread the toast with mayonnaise and top with the bacon, then layer the turkey, lettuce, and tomato over the bacon. Place the other bread slice on top, mayonnaise side down. Push a toothpick into each corner of the sandwich to hold it together. Cut in half or quarters. Serve with a side of sweet pickles.

Serves 2

Tuna Salad

Everyone should know how to make a great tuna salad. Try some of the Add-Ins suggested below until you find the right combination or come up with some of your own.

1 (6-ounce) can water-packed tuna

1 tablespoon mayonnaise

Adult Help Needed

1. Open the can of tuna, being careful with the sharp edges of the lid. Drain juices off in a strainer.

2. Place tuna in a medium bowl and break into small pieces with a fork. Stir in the mayonnaise and mix lightly with a fork until well blended. Spread the tuna salad on your favorite bread to make sandwiches. Serve with a glass of cold milk.

Serves 1 or 2

Add-Ins

Stir some of the following into the Tuna Salad if you like:

1 hard-boiled egg, chopped

1 celery stalk, finely chopped

1 teaspoon finely chopped onion

1 tablespoon sweet pickle relish

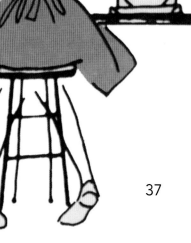

Blueberry Soup

If you want to surprise everyone with your cooking skills, serve this unusual soup. It is a refreshing way to enjoy blueberries. Because it isn't too sweet, you could serve it as the first course of a special meal or have it for dessert, topped with vanilla ice cream.

1 pint fresh blueberries or 2 cups frozen

5 tablespoons apple cider

2 tablespoons maple syrup

Pinch of ground allspice

Pinch of ground nutmeg

1. In a colander wash and drain the blueberries. Combine the blueberries, cider, maple syrup, allspice, and nutmeg in a medium saucepan.

Adult Help Needed

2. Turn the heat on high and bring to a boil, then reduce heat to low. Simmer for 10 minutes, stirring occasionally. Serve soup warm in small bowls. You can also cover and refrigerate for 1 hour and serve the soup chilled.

Serves 4

Chicken and Rice Soup

This is a filling soup and a good way to use leftover chicken.
Try adding in your favorite vegetables for a complete meal.

6 cups chicken broth

¼ cup uncooked rice

1 teaspoon salt

¼ teaspoon black pepper

½ cup cooked chicken, diced or shredded

½ cup carrots, chopped

1 stalk celery, finely diced

1 clove garlic, chopped

Adult Help Needed

1. Place the chicken broth in a medium saucepan. Turn the heat on medium-high and bring to a boil.

2. Add the uncooked rice, diced or shredded chicken, chopped vegetables, salt, and pepper to the broth. Cover pan with lid and simmer on low for 20 minutes. Serve in soup bowls and sprinkle Parmesan cheese on top. Serve with crackers or buttered toast.

Serves 2

Old-Fashioned Potato Soup

This potato soup recipe was my grandmother's, and I have always loved it. Serve with Surprise Corn Muffins (see page 108) for a hearty lunch or dinner.

6 russet potatoes (about 2 pounds)

2 tablespoons butter

1 slice bacon, chopped

1 small onion, finely chopped

1 stalk celery, finely chopped

2 tablespoons all-purpose flour

1½ teaspoons salt

Water (6 cups for boiling)

½ cup milk

1. Scrub the potatoes under cold running water using a vegetable brush. With a vegetable peeler, peel potatoes, then rinse again. Cut the potatoes in half, then chop them into small pieces.

2. Place the butter in a large saucepan and turn heat on medium-low. When the butter is melted, add the bacon, onion, and celery to the pan. Cook over medium-low heat, stirring, until the onions are just beginning to turn golden and the bacon is crisp. Add the flour and salt to the pan and stir to combine. (Adding the flour will thicken the soup as it cooks.)

3. Add potatoes to the pan with bacon, and fill with enough water (about 6 cups) to cover the potatoes. Turn the heat on high and bring to a boil. Reduce heat to medium-low. Simmer until potatoes are tender but not mushy, about 20 minutes. The potatoes should feel slightly firm if you poke a fork into them. Add the milk to the soup and simmer for 5 minutes. Ladle into bowls and serve hot. Add salt and pepper to taste.

Serves 4

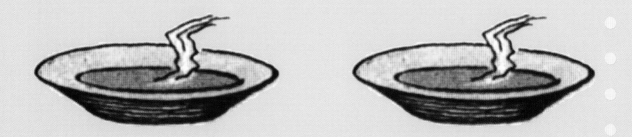

Easy Cheesy Broccoli Soup

This is a quick way to make a delicious and nutritious soup.
American cheese makes this soup velvety and smooth.

1 head of broccoli, washed, trimmed, and cut in small pieces

1 teaspoon salt

1 cup milk

½ pound sliced American cheese (about 16 slices)

Pepper and salt to taste

Adult Help Needed

1. Set a colander in the sink. Place the broccoli in a large saucepan and fill with cold water to cover the broccoli. Add salt to the water and turn the heat on high. Bring to a boil then reduce heat to medium-low and simmer until the broccoli is soft, about 15 minutes. Turn off heat. Using a pot holder, drain the broccoli in a colander.

2. In a blender, combine 1 cup of broccoli and ½ cup of milk. Cover with lid. Turn on blender to medium speed and blend until smooth. Pour the blended mixture back into the large saucepan. Continue to blend remaining milk and broccoli and add to the large saucepan.

3. Warm the broccoli mixture over a low heat until warm. Add the cheese slices and stir until completely melted. Add salt and pepper to taste. You can add ¼ cup milk for a thinner soup, and more cheese if you want it cheesier. Serve hot.

Serves 4

Emergency Soup

This 10-minute soup will save the day when you need a quick meal or a nourishing snack. This is also soothing when you have a cold.

2 cups canned chicken broth

½ cup uncooked egg noodles, or thin pasta

¼ cup fresh snowpeas or frozen baby peas

1 tablespoon Parmesan cheese

Adult Help Needed

1. Place the chicken broth in a medium saucepan. Turn the heat on medium-high and bring to a boil.

2. Add the egg noodles and peas and simmer until the noodles are tender, about 10 minutes. Ladle in a bowl and sprinkle with cheese. Serve with crackers or buttered toast.

Serves 1

Creamy Tomato Soup

My mother served us this soup on winter afternoons when we came in from ice skating. It is delicious on its own, or serve it with Grilled Cheese (see page 34) for a classic lunch. The little bit of onion and thyme makes this soup extra flavorful.

½ teaspoon finely minced onion

2 tablespoons butter

3 tablespoons flour

1½ tablespoons sugar

1 teaspoon salt

2 cups tomato juice concentrate

1½ cups cold milk

Pinch of fresh or dried thyme (optional)

Adult Help Needed

1. Peel and chop the onion very fine. In a large saucepan, melt butter over medium-low heat until completely melted. Add onion and cook, stirring, until onion begins to turn clear, 2 to 3 minutes. Don't brown the onions—they need to remain soft and clear.

2. Stir in the flour, sugar, and salt. Whisk until completely blended. Slowly add the tomato juice, whisking constantly. Be sure to stir the bottom and sides of the pan so that all of the flour mixture is well blended. Simmer for 1 minute, or until the mixture thickens. Add the milk to the saucepan and stir until smooth and creamy. Let the mixture cook another 3 minutes. Add a pinch of fresh or dried thyme for extra flavor. Serve hot.

Serves 4

Eggs for Breakfast, Lunch, or Supper

Poached Egg

Scrambled Eggs

Knothole Egg

Eggs on a Raft

Cheese Omelet

Hard-Boiled Eggs

Egg Salad

Deviled Eggs

Perfect Fried Egg Sandwich

Creamed Eggs on Toast

White Sauce

Poached Egg

The simple trick to poaching an egg is simmering it very gently on a low heat.
Within 3 minutes you will have a perfectly cooked egg.

1 egg

1 slice buttered toast

Salt and pepper to taste

Adult Help Needed

1. Toast and butter the bread. Put on a serving plate and set aside.

2. Fill a small, deep skillet with water. Bring the water to a boil over medium-high heat, then turn down heat to low. (The water should be simmering.) Break the egg into a small cup. Carefully pour the egg into simmering water. The egg will immediately start to cook. Let it simmer for 3 minutes. (Stay close to your egg; it poaches quickly!)

3. When the white of the egg is firm, turn off the heat. Use a slotted spoon to lift the egg from the water. Let it drain in the spoon, then place it on the buttered toast, or serve it in a small bowl with the toast on the side for dipping. Sprinkle with salt and pepper to taste.

Serves 1

Add-Ins

Try adding 1 teaspoon of white vinegar to the water. It will help to keep the egg white in a compact shape, but don't worry—your egg won't taste like vinegar!

Scrambled Eggs

If you can scramble eggs (and it's really easy), you'll be able to make breakfast, lunch, or supper for your family. For variety, add 2 tablespoon of shredded Cheddar cheese or chopped ham to the egg mixture before cooking.

4 eggs

1 tablespoon water

1 tablespoons unsalted butter

½ teaspoon salt

Black pepper to taste

Adult Help Needed

1. Break the eggs into a medium bowl. Add the water, salt, pepper, and then beat the eggs with a fork or wire whisk until thoroughly mixed, about 30 seconds.

2. Heat a medium skillet over medium-low heat. Add the butter and melt completely. Using a pot holder, tilt the skillet so the butter covers the bottom. Add the egg mixture and stir with a fork until the eggs begin to form soft lumps.

3. When the eggs are the consistency you like, turn off the heat. Use a pot holder to remove the pan from heat. Spoon the eggs onto serving plates.

Serves 2 or 3

Knothole Egg

This recipe reminds some people of a hole in the side of a tree called a knothole. It's a fun breakfast for days when you need extra brain power, like before taking a test. It's also a perfect weekend supper or nutritious snack.

1 slice bread

1 tablespoon butter

1 egg

Salt and pepper to taste

Adult Help Needed

1. Using a small drinking glass or a round cookie cutter, cut a hole in the center of the bread. Remove the cut-out circle of bread. (You can fry this piece later.)

2. In a small skillet melt the butter over medium-low heat. Place bread in skillet and crack the egg into the hole in the bread. Cook until the underside of the toast is golden, about 5 minutes, then, with a spatula, flip the egg and toast. Cook until the other side is nicely browned, about 3 minutes. Use the spatula to slide the egg and toast out of the pan onto a serving plate. Serve hot.

Serves 1

Eggs on a Raft

This is one of our family's favorite egg breakfasts and emergency dinners.

1 whole wheat English muffin, split in half

2 tablespoons Cream cheese, softened

1 tablespoon butter

2 eggs

Salt and pepper to taste

Adult Help Needed

1. Toast the English muffin halves until golden brown. With a butter knife, spread the Cream cheese evenly on each muffin half. Put on a serving plate and set aside.

2. Heat a medium skillet over medium-low heat. Add the butter and melt. Break eggs, one at a time, directly into the skillet. (Be careful not to break the yolks.) Cook for 4 minutes, or until the egg whites are crisp along the edges. With a spatula, remove the eggs from the pan and place on the toasted muffin halves. Sprinkle with salt and pepper. You will want to eat this with a knife and fork.

Serves 1 or 2

Cheese Omelet

Making an omelet is easy, but it can take several tries to get it just right, so be prepared to practice on friends and family. And don't worry —even the mistakes will taste delicious!

3 eggs

1 tablespoon water

¼ teaspoon salt

1 tablespoon butter

¼ teaspoon black pepper

2 tablespoons Cheddar cheese, shredded

1. Break the eggs into a small bowl. Add the water and salt, then beat with a fork or wire whisk for 30 seconds or until the yolks and whites are well blended.

2. In a small skillet melt the butter over medium-high heat. As the butter begins to melt, use a pot holder to tilt the skillet to spread the butter around the bottom and sides. When the butter is bubbling, add the eggs.

3. Once the eggs start to set, use a rubber spatula to lift the outer edge of the eggs gently toward the center of the pan. (This allows the uncooked eggs to run underneath the cooked part of the eggs.) Do this several times, on all sides, until the eggs are firm and no longer runny. Add the cheese, in an even layer, to the center of the omelet.

4. Use the spatula to loosen the omelet underneath, then fold the omelet over to form a semicircle. Using a pot holder, hold the handle of the pan and tilt it to slide the omelet onto the plate. Serve right away.

Serves 1 or 2

Add-Ins

Swiss cheese, grated

Cream cheese

Diced ham

Asparagus tips, cooked and chopped

Broccoli, cooked and chopped

Peas, fresh or frozen

Potatoes, cooked and chopped

Spinach, cooked and chopped

Fresh tomatoes, chopped

Zucchini, diced or grated

Hard-Boiled Eggs

You can store hard-boiled eggs in the refrigerator, unpeeled, for one week.

Place the eggs in a saucepan large enough to hold the eggs in one layer on the bottom. Add enough cold water to cover the eggs by 1 inch. Bring water to a boil over high heat. When the water is boiling and bubbling, turn heat to low and simmer eggs for 12 minutes. Using a pot holder, remove saucepan from the heat and drain the eggs. Immediately refill the pan with cold water. Let the eggs sit in the water until cool. Drain in a colander.

Peeling Hard-Boiled Eggs

Tap the cooled egg gently on the countertop to crack the shell all over. Peel off the shells with your finger tips. Running the eggs under cold water while peeling will help keep them clean. Place peeled eggs on a plate to dry.

Egg Salad

Nothing is easier to make and more delicious to eat than a simple egg salad. Try adding in chopped celery, onion, and relish to this basic recipe.

4 Hard-Boiled Eggs (see page 54)

3 tablespoons light mayonnaise

¼ teaspoon salt

Black pepper to taste

Adult Help Needed

Peel the Hard-Boiled Eggs under cold running water as directed on page 54. Cut the eggs in quarters and put them in a medium bowl. Mash the eggs with a fork until they are in small pieces. Stir in the mayonnaise. Mix well. Add salt and pepper to taste. Serve the egg salad on a bed of lettuce or on sandwich bread.

Serves 2

Add-Ins

1 stalk celery, chopped fine

1 tablespoon sweet pickle relish

1 teaspoon onion, chopped fine

Deviled Eggs

Not just for picnics, these little egg boats are nice for lunch or snacks. To pack deviled eggs for a lunchbox or a picnic, put 2 halves together, yolk to yolk, and wrap in waxed paper, twisting the ends of the paper to secure it.

6 Hard-Boiled Eggs, peeled (see page 54)

2 tablespoons light mayonnaise

2 teaspoon Prepared yellow mustard

¼ teaspoon salt

Pinch of black pepper

Paprika for garnish

Adult Help Needed

1. Peel the eggs as directed on page 54 and cut them in half lengthwise. Carefully slip out the yolk into a small bowl, and place egg white halves on a plate.

2. Mix in the mayonnaise, mustard, salt, and pepper. Mash with a fork until smooth and creamy.

3. Using a teaspoon, fill the egg white halves with the yolk mixture. Sprinkle with paprika and chill in the refrigerator.

Makes 12 halves

Perfect Fried Egg Sandwich

Mustard, salt, pepper, and untoasted bread are the simple secret ingredients for a perfect fried egg sandwich.

1 tablespoon butter

1 egg

2 slices multigrain bread

Salt and pepper to taste

1 teaspoon Prepared yellow mustard, or to taste

Adult Help Needed

1. Place 2 slices of bread on a plate. Heat a small skillet over medium heat. Add the butter and melt.

2. Meanwhile, crack the egg into a small dish. When butter is melted and beginning to bubble, add egg to the skillet. Use a spatula to flatten out the yolk so it spreads around, but don't scramble the egg.

3. Fry the egg until the edges start to brown lightly and look crisp, about 4 minutes. With the spatula, flip the egg and fry until the underside is crisp and brown, about 3 minutes.

4. Use the spatula to place the cooked egg on top of 1 slice. Salt and pepper the egg to taste. With a butter knife, spread mustard over the egg. Place the other slice of bread on top. Cut the sandwich in half and serve right away.

Serves 1

Creamed Eggs on Toast

This is an old-fashioned dish that is certain to be a family favorite again. Serve sliced Hard-Boiled Eggs on toast topped with warm White Sauce sprinkled with nutmeg. Try this for lunch or supper.

½ cup White Sauce (see page 59)

2 Hard-Boiled Eggs (see page 54)

2 slices bread

2 teaspoon butter

Adult Help Needed

1. Warm the White Sauce over a low heat in a small saucepan. Peel the eggs as directed on page 54.

2. Toast and butter the bread. Place each slice of buttered toast on a plate. Slice the eggs and divide between the toast slices. Pour warm sauce over eggs.

Serves 2

White Sauce

This traditional sauce has many uses and is worth learning to make. Be sure to add warm, almost hot, milk to the cooked butter-and-flour mixture. This will help keep the sauce smooth and creamy.

1 cup milk

2 tablespoons butter

2 tablespoons all-purpose flour

¼ teaspoon salt

Pinch of black pepper

Pinch of ground nutmeg

Adult Help Needed

1. Place milk in a small saucepan and heat over medium-low until hot but not boiling. (You will see steam rising off the surface of the milk.) Turn off heat and use pot holder to pour milk into a liquid measuring cup. Set aside.

2. In a medium saucepan, melt the butter over medium-low heat. Add the flour to the butter and use a wire whisk to blend until smooth and slightly bubbly. Holding the small saucepan with a pot holder, slowly pour the milk into the mixture. Whisk the mixture to blend. (You don't have to add all the milk at once.) When all of the milk has been added, continue to whisk over a medium-low heat until you have a smooth white sauce. Stir in salt, pepper, and nutmeg. Serve warm.

Makes 1 cup

Salads and Vegetable Dishes

Melon Drops

✳

Summer Berry Fruit Cups

✳

Crunchy Apple Salad

✳

Carrot Raisin Salad

✳

Everyday Vinaigrette

✳

Simple Green Salad

✳

Four Seasons Salad

✳

Creamy Dressing

✳

Carrot Curls

✳

Buttered Green Beans

✳

Roasted Asparagus

✳

Corn on the Cob

✳

Corn off the Cob

✳

Baked Acorn Squash

✳

Spicy Sweet Potato Wedges

✳

Baked Potatoes

✳

Smashed Potatoes

✳

Potato Pancakes

✳

Glazed Carrots

Melon Drops

Using the melon halves as bowls is a fun way to serve fruit if you are making a special brunch or lunch.

1 honeydew melon, or cantaloupe

2 tablespoons honey

2 tablespoons plain yogurt

2 tablespoons fresh lime juice

Adult Help Needed

1. Cut the melon in half. Scoop out the seeds and discard. Using melon baller or a small spoon, scoop flesh out of each melon half. Place melon balls in a large bowl as you scoop. You should have about 24 melon balls. Set aside the hollowed-out melon halves.

2. In a small bowl combine honey, yogurt, and lime juice. Whisk with a fork until smooth. Spoon mixture over fruit and stir gently. Spoon fruit into reserved melon halves. Serve chilled.

Serves 4

Summer Berry Fruit Cups

This berry salad is especially good in the summer when the fruits are in season. Be sure to wash fresh berries just before using. Damp berries can get soft and even moldy if they sit too long. A small sprinkling of sugar helps to bring out the berry flavors.

1 pint fresh blueberries

1 pint fresh raspberries

1 pint fresh strawberries

¼ cup orange juice

½ teaspoon granulated sugar

Mint leaves (optional)

1. Gently rinse the blueberries, raspberries, and strawberries in a colander and drain well. Place the washed fruit in a large bowl. Sprinkle with the sugar. Add the orange juice and toss lightly with a spoon until mixed. (The berries are delicate and will get smashed if you stir too much.)

2. Cover bowl and chill in the refrigerator for ½ hour. Spoon berries into small glasses or cups to serve. Garnish each serving with a mint leaf.

Serves 4

Crunchy Apple Salad

This is a wonderful salad for beginning cooks. Add a handful of chopped walnuts if you prefer a crunchier salad.

2 to 3 apples

1 cup grapes, halved

1 stalk celery, chopped in small pieces

¼ cup light mayonnaise or plain low-fat yogurt

1 teaspoon fresh lemon juice

Adult Help Needed

1. Cut apples into quarters. Use a paring knife to cut off the peels, and remove the cores. Cut the apples into bite-size chunks. You should have about 2 cups. Place in a serving bowl. Stir the celery and grapes into the apples.

2. In a small bowl, combine the mayonnaise or yogurt and lemon juice. Stir until well blended. Pour over the apple mixture. Stir gently until the mayonnaise coats the apples. Add another tablespoon of mayonnaise or yogurt for a thicker sauce. Cover bowl and refrigerate until chilled. Serve as a side dish or spoon salad onto a bed of crisp lettuce leaves and serve.

Serves 4

Carrot Raisin Salad

Carrots and raisins make a sweet and healthy combination that's easy to make. Even the youngest cooks can help prepare this favorite salad.

3 tablespoons orange juice

Pinch of ground nutmeg

½ cup raisins

3 large carrots

1 tablespoon light olive oil

1. In a medium bowl combine the orange juice and nutmeg. Add the raisins and let soak while you prepare the carrots. (This will make them plump and juicy.)

Adult Help Needed

2. Peel the carrots, then grate using the large tear-drop holes of a box grater. Hold the grater with one hand and grate the food in the front of the grater. Keep your fingers on the outside, away from the holes. Add carrots to the raisin mixture. Stir in olive oil and mix well. Cover bowl and refrigerate until chilled.

Serves 2 or 3

Everyday Vinaigrette

*A good dressing begins with olive oil and the right amount
tartness from vinegar. Experiment to find the right balance of flavors you like.*

6 tablespoons olive oil

1 tablespoon lemon juice

1 tablespoon red wine vinegar

½ teaspoon salt

¼ teaspoon pepper

Combine all the ingredients in a glass jar. Screw the lid on tightly and
shake, until well mixed. Taste test by dipping a clean lettuce leaf into
the dressing. If you want it tarter, add a little more vinegar or lemon
juice. If it is too tart, add some more oil or a teaspoon of water. When
ready to use, shake again and spoon or pour over salad.

Makes about ½ cup

Simple Green Salad

To make a great green salad, start with a really fresh lettuce. There are many varieties available in local stores and at farmers markets. Lettuce should be crisp and firm, so don't use wilted or brown leaves.

8 cups greens, such as Buttercrunch, Romaine, Iceberg

¼ cup Everyday Vinaigrette (see page 66)

1. To prepare the lettuce remove damaged or wilted leaves. Separate the lettuce leaves and wash under cold running water. If the lettuce is very sandy, swish it around in a bowl of cold water to loosen all the dirt, then let it sit in the water for a few minutes. Repeat rinsing until the lettuce is clean, and there is no grit or sand in the bottom of the bowl. Lift the lettuce out and drain well.

2. Tear the leaves in bite-size pieces and place on a clean dry towel. Carefully pat the leaves dry to remove all water. Wet leaves will dilute the dressing. (You can also use a salad spinner to clean and dry lettuce.)

3. When ready to serve, place lettuce in a salad bowl. Pour 2 or 3 tablespoons of dressing over the leaves. Using a large fork and spoon, toss gently until the dressing coats the lettuce. Add more dressing as needed. Serve on salad plates.

Serves 2 to 4

BUTTER

Four Seasons Salad

The best salads use fruits and vegetables when they are in season. Mix and match according to the time of year. Most salad ingredients can be served raw but items such as brussels sprouts, squash and potatoes need to be cooked in advance. Simple Vinagrette (see page 66) or Creamy Dressing (see page 69) works with most combination of ingredients.

Spring

Artichokes, asparagus tips, avocados, lettuce, carrots, collard greens, green onions, new potatoes, pineapples, spinach, sugar snap peas

Summer

Apricots, beets, berries (assorted), broccoli, brussels sprouts, celery, cherry tomatoes, sweet corn, cucumbers, eggplant, green beans, green onions, green peas, green, red and yellow peppers, lettuce, mangos, melons (assorted), radishes, summer squash, spinach, tomatoes, waxed beans, zucchini

Fall

Acorn squash, apples, beets, broccoli, brussels sprouts, cabbage, carrots, cauliflower, pears, pumpkin, spinach, sugar snap peas, yams

Winter

Artichokes, avocados, beets, bok choy, broccoli, brussels sprouts, cabbage, cauliflower, carrots, celery, grapefruit, kale, lettuce, oranges, potatoes, parsnips, radishes, rutabaga, snow peas, butternut squash, sweet potatoes, turnips, yams

Creamy Dressing

This dressing goes well with freshly sliced cucumbers as well as fresh lettuce.

2 tablespoons cider vinegar

1 teaspoon sugar

½ teaspoon salt

½ cup light sour cream (or plain yogurt)

In a small bowl combine the vinegar, sugar, and salt. Stir until the sugar and salt are dissolved, then add the sour cream and combine until smooth. Taste the dressing to adjust the sweet and sour taste. Spoon dressing over sliced cucumbers or lettuce to taste. Serve chilled.

Carrot Curls

Keep these little curls on hand in the refrigerator to serve alongside a sandwich or a snack. Dip carrot curls in a Creamy Dressing (recipe above).

1 large carrot, washed and peeled

Draw a vegetable peeler lengthwise down a peeled carrot until you have a thin strip of carrot. Place carrot strips in a bowl of ice water until strips curl. Cover bowl and refrigerate.
Use as needed.

Serves 1 or 2

Buttered Green Beans

This method of cooking fresh green beans works every time. They turn out nicely salted and tender but not too soft. Be sure to select beans that are crisp and green, not wilted.

½ pound fresh green beans

1 tablespoon salt for cooking, plus extra for serving

1 tablespoon butter or olive oil

Adult Help Needed

1. Wash the beans in a colander under cold running water. Snap off both ends of the bean with your fingers. Fill a large saucepan with water and bring to a boil over a medium-high heat.

2. Add salt to water. (The water might stop boiling for a few seconds.) When it begins to boil again, add beans and cover with a lid. Boil the beans for 8 minutes. The cooked beans should be firm and slightly crunchy.

3. Using a pot holder, remove pan from the heat. Drain the beans in a colander. Placed cooked beans in a serving bowl. Add butter or olive oil and salt to taste, then gently stir. Serve right away.

Serves 2 to 3

Roasted Asparagus

Roasting asparagus in the oven is a delicious way to prepare this spring vegetable. The melted cheese on top makes it extra flavorful. If the asparagus is very fresh and tender, you don't have to peel the skin.

1 pound fresh asparagus

1 tablepoon olive oil

½ teaspoon salt

1 tablespoon grated Parmesan cheese

Adult Help Needed

1. Place rack in the middle of the oven. Preheat oven to 400 degrees.

2. Trim tough ends from the asparagus spears. Place spears in a bowl. Add the oil and toss gently to coat asparagus. Spread asparagus on a lightly greased baking sheet in a single layer. Sprinkle asparagus spears with salt and Parmesan cheese.

3. Roast until the spears are tender when pricked with a tip of a knife, about 15 minutes, depending on their thickness. Using oven mitts, remove the baking sheet from the oven. Set on a wire rack to cool. With a spatula, place asparagus on plates and serve right away.

Serves 4

Corn on the Cob

The fresher the corn, the better the corn on the cob. Buy produce from local farm stands or farmers market, or ask your grocer if they carry locally grown produce. We often make corn on the cob our main course for a summer supper and then everyone gets two or three ears.

4 ears corn, shucked and cleaned

Butter

Salt and black pepper to taste

1. Shuck the corn by pulling off the green husks. Remove all the silky strands that stick to the corn kernels. Discard the husks and silks. Place the cleaned ears on a serving plate.

Adult Help Needed

2. Place a vegetable steamer on the bottom of a large pot. Add enough water to come just below the vegetable steamer. Place the ears of corn in the pot. Place the lid on top.

3. Turn the heat high and bring water to a boil, then turn down to medium-low and let the corn steam for 8 minutes. Turn off the heat and let the corn steam for another 2 minutes with the lid on.

4. Using a pot holder, remove the lid. Using tongs, remove the cooked ears of corn and place on platter. Serve hot. Add butter, salt, and pepper to taste.

Serves 2 to 4

Corn off the Cob

This recipe uses leftover corn on the cob to make a side dish.
You might want to cook extra corn just for this dish.

4 cooked ears of corn

3 tablespoons milk

2 tablespoon butter

½ teaspoon salt

¼ teaspoon pepper

Adult Help Needed

1. Using cooled ears, snap each ear in half and place on a cutting board. Hold the top upright and run knife along the length of the corn and cut off the kernels. (They will fall off easily in little bunches because they are already cooked.) Rotate the cob and continue scraping until the corn is clean of its kernels.

2. Place the corn kernels in a small saucepan and add the milk and butter. Cook over medium-low heat until the butter is melted and the corn is hot, about 5 minutes. Stir in the salt and pepper. Using a pot holder, remove pan from the heat. Serve right away.

Baked Acorn Squash

Real maple syrup and thyme are the secret ingredients in this recipe.

1 acorn squash

2 tablespoons butter

2 teaspoons real maple syrup

¼ teaspoon salt

¼ teaspoon black pepper

Pinch of fresh or dried thyme

Adult Help Needed

1. Place rack in the middle of the oven. Preheat oven to 400 degrees. Place a sheet of aluminum foil on the bottom of baking sheet or a 9-inch square pan.

2. Have an adult cut the squash in half, lengthwise. Cut through the stem end rather than crosswise. Scoop the seeds out of each half with a spoon and discard. Place hollowed out halves with the cut side up in a prepared dish.

3. In each squash hollow, place 1 tablespoon of the butter, and 1 teaspoon of the maple syrup. Sprinkle half of the salt, pepper, and thyme in each hollow. Bake for 1 hour, or until tender. Using oven mitts, remove the pan from oven. Let cool for 5 minutes before serving.

Serves 2

Spicy Sweet Potato Wedges

Serve these oven fries as a side dish with Mini Meat Loaves (see page 82).

2 large sweet potatoes

1 tablespoons olive oil

½ teaspoon salt

½ teaspoon mild chili powder

¼ teaspoon black pepper, or to taste

**Adult
Help
Needed**

1. Place rack in the middle of the oven. Preheat oven to 400 degrees. Place a sheet of aluminum foil on the bottom of baking sheet.

2. Scrub sweet potatoes well under cold running water using a vegetable brush. Pat dry with clean dish towel. With adult help, cut the potato in half lengthwise, then cut each half into 6 wedges.

3. Place the potatoes in a large bowl. Add the oil, salt, chili powder, and black pepper and toss until the potatoes are evenly coated. Arrange in a single layer on a baking sheet. Bake for 20 minutes. Using oven mitts, remove the baking sheet from the oven. Use a spatula to turn the fries, then return baking sheet to oven to bake 10 minutes longer, or until crisp and brown. Serve hot.

Serves 2 to 3

Baked Potatoes

Once you learn how to bake a potato, you'll always have the basis of an easy lunch or dinner. Top with sour cream and chives, crumbled bacon, shredded Cheddar cheese.

2 large russet potatoes (also known as baking potatoes)

2 teaspoons butter or olive oil

Salt to taste

Pepper to taste

Adult Help Needed

1. Place rack in the middle of the oven. Preheat oven to 400 degrees.

2. Scrub the potatoes under cold running water using a vegetable brush. Use a fork to poke several holes in the potatoes. (This helps the moisture and hot steam escape when cooking.) Using an oven mitt, place potatoes directly on the oven rack. Bake for 1 hour, or until tender.

3. Using oven mitts, remove potatoes from the oven. Use a butter knife to cut a slit lengthwise in the top of each potato. (Be careful because the potatoes are very hot and escaping steam can burn you.) Place 1 teaspoon of butter or oil inside each slit. Sprinkle with salt, and pepper to taste. Serve hot.

Serves 2

Smashed Potatoes

Use a hand-held potato masher instead of an electric mixer because the texture should be a little lumpy and not perfectly smooth. Save any leftovers for Potato Pancakes (see page 78).

1¼ pounds red-skinned potatoes (about 10 small potatoes)

¾ cup milk

2 tablespoons butter or olive oil

½ teaspoon salt

Pepper to taste

Adult Help Needed

1. Scrub the potatoes under cold running water using a vegetable brush. Pat dry with clean dish towel. Do not peel the potatoes. Place in a large saucepan. Add just enough water to cover the potatoes. Bring to a boil over high heat and then turn heat to low. Simmer potatoes until tender, about 25 minutes. Test for doneness by carefully poking a fork into a potato. If it still firm, let it boil a little longer. With a pot holder, remove pan from heat.

2. Have an adult help drain the potatoes in a colander. Let the potatoes drain for a few minutes, then return them to the pot. Slowly add milk and butter or oil to potatoes and mash with a potato masher until you are pleased with the texture. Add salt and pepper to taste. Serve right away.

Serves 4

Potato Pancakes

This is a great way to use leftover Smashed Potatoes (see page 77). Combine the eggs and milk with the potatoes, then cook the pancakes in butter until they are brown and crispy. Try them for breakfast topped with sour cream and a side of homemade Spicy Applesauce (see page 132).

2 cup leftover Smashed Potatoes

2 eggs

3 tablespoons butter or olive oil

Adult Help Needed

1. Place the Smashed Potatoes in a medium-size bowl. Beat in the egg and milk until well combined.

2. Heat the butter or oil in a medium skillet over medium-low. Drop spoonfuls (about ¼ cup each) of the potato mixture into the skillet. Use the back of the spoon to shape the potato mixture into patties. Cook until undersides are crisp and golden brown, about 4 minutes. Using a spatula, flip the pancakes and cook until the other sides are golden brown, about 4 minutes. Place cooked pancakes on a plate and serve right away. Serves warm.

Serves 2 to 4

Glazed Carrots

You will be surprised how flavorful and delicious carrots are when cooked in a little butter and sugar.

1 pound bag baby carrots

¼ cup water, more if needed

1 tablespoon butter

½ teaspoon sugar

¼ teaspoon salt

Freshly ground pepper, to taste

Adult Help Needed

1. Place the carrots in a medium saucepan in one layer, not stacked. Place the butter in the pan and sprinkle with sugar, and salt.

2. Pour water in the pan so that it comes halfway up the sides of the carrots. Cover the pan with a lid. Bring carrots to a boil over medium high heat and then simmer on a low heat, for about 15 minutes. When all of the water has evaporated, check for doneness by carefully poking a fork into the middle of the carrots. Using a pot holder, remove pan from the heat. Serve warm.

Serves 4

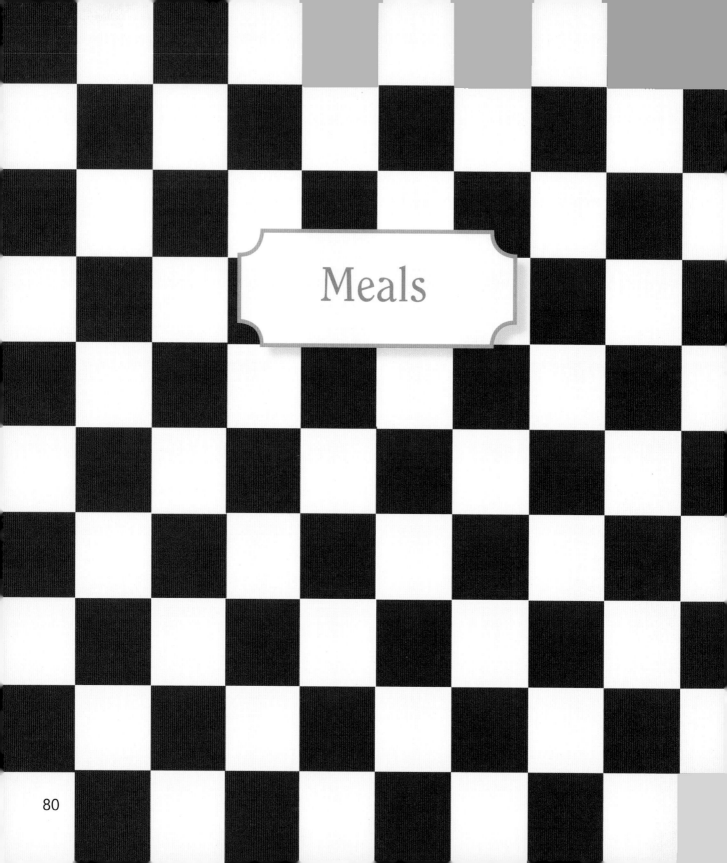

Meals

Mini Meat Loaves

✳

Homemade Bread Crumbs

✳

Tomato Sauce

✳

Spaghetti and Meatballs

✳

Yummy Turkey Meatballs

✳

Pigs in the Poke

✳

Ham and Ginger Ale

✳

Chicken Tenders

✳

Lemon Honey Mustard Sauce

✳

Quick and Thick Barbecued Drumsticks

✳

Crusty Fish Fillets

✳

Creamy Macaroni and Cheese

✳

Ohio Sloppy Joe

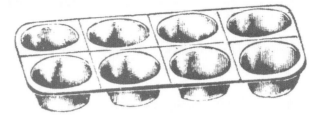

Mini Meat Loaves

These mini loaves will make dinner seem like a party!

2 slices soft bread

¼ cup milk

1 egg

1 small yellow onion, finely chopped

1 pound lean ground beef

1 tablespoon ketchup

½ teaspoon salt

¼ teaspoon black pepper

**Adult
Help
Needed**

1. Set the rack in the middle of the oven. Preheat oven to 350 degrees. Use vegetable oil to lightly grease a 6-cup muffin tin. Use a paper napkin to spread the oil evenly inside each muffin cup.

2. Tear the bread slices into small pieces and place in a medium bowl. Add the milk and let the bread soak until most of the milk is absorbed.

3. Peel an onion and grate into the bowl using the medium-size holes of a box grater. (Be careful not to scrape your fingers as you do this.) Discard the remaining onion when it gets too small to scrape.

4. Crack the egg into the bowl with the bread and onions. Add the beef, ketchup, salt, and pepper. Using clean hands or a large spoon, gently mix until well combined.

5. Divide the meat mixture among the 6 muffin cups. Smooth the top of each.

6. Place muffin pan in oven and bake for 40 minutes. Using oven mitts remove the pan from oven. Let the meat loaves cool for a few minutes. Run a fork around the edge of each meat loaf, then lift it out of the pan onto a serving plate (serves 2 loaves per person).

Serves 3

Homemade Bread Crumbs

Don't throw away day-old bread. Save it to make your own bread crumbs. Put dried bread pieces in the blender and cover with lid. Turn on medium speed and chop fine. Store the crumbs in a plastic container or plastic bag in freezer until ready to use.

Tomato Sauce

Homemade tomato sauce is a must for spaghetti and meatballs.
If you are in a pinch for time, use store-bought sauce.

1 (32-ounce) can peeled plum tomatoes

¼ cup olive oil

1 tablespoon butter

2 large garlic cloves, finely chopped

1 tablespoon fresh chopped parsley, leaves only

1 teaspoon salt

½ teaspoon black pepper

Pinch of sugar

1 tablespoon tomato paste

Adult Help Needed

1. Drain the tomatoes and place in a bowl. With clean hands, mash into smaller pieces. Set aside.

2. Combine the olive oil and butter in a large saucepan. Turn heat on medium-low and stir until the butter is melted. Add the garlic, parsley, salt, pepper, and sugar. Cook, stirring occasionally with a wooden spoon, for 5 minutes.

3. Add the tomatoes and tomato paste to the saucepan and cook for 30 minutes. Using a pot holder, remove from heat and use sauce however you like. Store extra sauce in lidded jar or plastic container in refrigerator.

Makes about 4 or 5 cups

Spaghetti and Meatballs

2 quarts (8 cups) cold water

1 teaspoon salt

½ pound spaghetti

Yummy Turkey Meatballs (see page 86)

Parmesan cheese, to taste

Adult Help Needed

1. Fill a large, heavy pot halfway with 2 quarts (8 cups) of cold water. Turn heat on high and bring water to a rolling boil. Add the salt and spaghetti to the boiling water and cook for about 12 minutes, or until done to your taste. Stir occasionally with long wooden spoon or fork to keep the spaghetti from sticking together.

2. Set a colander in the sink. With adult help, use oven mitts or a pot holder to remove pot from heat. Pour contents of the pot away from you and into a colander, and drain well. Put the spaghetti in a large serving bowl. Pour warm Tomato Sauce and Yummy Turkey Meatballs over Spaghetti and toss. Serve warm with freshly grated Parmesan cheese.

Serves about 4 to 6

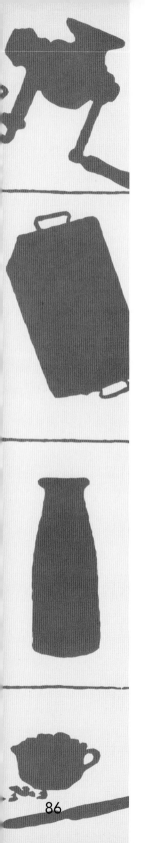

Yummy Turkey Meatballs

My brother Jay's oven-baked meatballs are delicious. Serve them to a crowd with Tomato Sauce (see page 84) for snacking or serve with Spaghetti (see page 85) for a fabulous family meal.

1 tablespoon vegetable oil (for greasing the pan)

1 egg

5 tablespoons grated Pecorino-Romano cheese

¼ cup Homemade Bread Crumbs (see page 83)

3 tablespoons ketchup

¼ teaspoon salt

¼ teaspoon black pepper

1 pound ground turkey

3 garlic cloves, chopped fine

¼ cup onion, chopped fine

2 cups Tomato Sauce (see page 84)

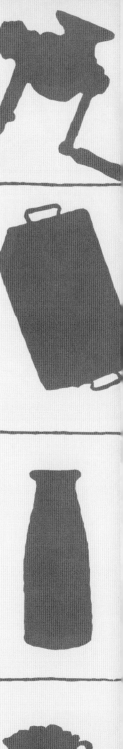

Adult Help Needed

1. Set the rack in the middle of the oven. Preheat oven to 350 degrees. Use vegetable oil to grease a baking sheet or shallow baking pan.

2. Combine the egg, grated cheese, bread crumbs, ketchup, salt, and pepper in a bowl. Add the turkey and mix with clean hands or large spoon until well combined.

3. Peel and chop fine the garlic cloves and add to mixture. Peel an onion and grate into the bowl using the medium-size holes of a box grater. (Be careful not to scrape your fingers as you do this.)

4. With clean hands, shape the turkey mixture into balls, about 2 inches across. Arrange about ½ inch apart in the prepared pan. Bake for 25 minutes, or until browned. (You don't need to turn these meatballs.)

5. Using oven mitts, remove pan from oven. Set on a rack to cool. Pour Tomato Sauce (see page 84) into a medium saucepan and use tongs or spatula to place meatballs in the sauce. Turn heat on medium-low and cook until sauce thickens and flavors blend together. Transfer meatballs and sauce to a serving bowl and serve with toothpicks or over Spaghetti (see page 85).

Makes 15 meatballs

Pigs in the Poke

This dish will cause a sensation when the popover batter rises high.
Serve with a dish of hot bubbling baked beans.

6 all-beef hot dogs

1 cup milk

2 eggs

2 tablespoons vegetable oil

1 cup all-purpose flour

½ teaspoon salt

Adult Help Needed

1. Set the rack in the middle of the oven. Preheat oven to 400 degrees. Lightly oil an 8-inch square baking dish. Cut each hot dog in 4 equal pieces and place evenly in a single layer in the baking dish.

2. In a medium bowl combine the milk, eggs, and oil. Using an electric mixer, slowly beat in the flour and salt, mixing until the batter is smooth and well blended, about 3 minutes. Pour batter over the hot dogs in the baking dish. Bake for 40 minutes, or until popover batter is high and golden.

3. Using oven mitts, remove the pan from oven. Serve right away. Use a spatula or spoon to serve.

Serves 4

Ham and Ginger Ale

The sauce for this dish has a surprise ingredient!

¼ cup brown sugar

1½ tablespoons Prepared mustard

½ teaspoon ground cloves

1 tablespoon butter

1 (1 pound) ham steak about ½ inch thick

¼ cup ginger ale

Adult Help Needed

1. In a small bowl combine the brown sugar, mustard, and cloves.

2. In a large skillet melt the butter over medium-high heat. Add ham steak and fry, turning with a spatula or fork, until lightly browned on both sides, about 8 minutes.

3. Using a pastry brush or a teaspoon, spread brown sugar mixture over ham (still in the skillet). Slowly pour the ginger ale into the skillet and stir. Simmer over low heat for another 3 minutes. Transfer ham to a platter and spoon the warm sauce on top. Serve with Smashed Potatoes (see page 77) and Buttered Green Beans (see page 70).

Serves 4

Chicken Tenders

These crisp morsels will quickly become a favorite meal. Be sure to make plenty of Lemon Honey Mustard Sauce (see page 91) for dipping!

1 tablespoon vegetable oil (for greasing the pan)

1 pound skinless chicken cutlets

1 cup grated Parmesan cheese

¼ teaspoon salt

¼ teaspoon black pepper

1 egg

Adult Help Needed

1. Set the rack in the middle of the oven. Preheat oven to 375 degrees. Line a large baking sheet or shallow baking dish with aluminum foil.

2. On a plastic cutting board cut the chicken into pieces about 2 inches square. Set the chicken aside and wash your hands with warm soapy water.

3. Combine the Parmesan cheese, salt, and pepper in a large resealable plastic bag. Set aside.

4. Crack the egg in a shallow bowl and beat lightly. Add chicken pieces to the egg. Use a fork and stir to coat completely. Place chicken pieces in the bag with cheese. Reseal the bag and shake to coat. (You can work in batches if necessary.)

5. Place coated chicken pieces on the prepared baking sheet. Place the baking sheet in the oven and bake until the chicken is crisp and golden, about 20 minutes. Using oven mitts, remove pan from the oven. Serve the chicken hot with Lemon Honey Mustard Sauce on the side, for dipping.

Serves 2 or 3

Lemon Honey Mustard Sauce

3 tablespoons honey

3 tablespoons Dijon-style mustard

1 teaspoon fresh lemon juice

Combine the honey, mustard, and lemon juice in a small bowl and stir well. Serve sauce at room temperature with Chicken Tenders, or cover and store in refrigerator until ready to use.

Serves 2 or 3

Quick and Thick Barbecued Drumsticks

½ cup ketchup

1 tablespoon molasses

1 tablespoon brown sugar

1½ teaspoon Dijon-style mustard

1½ teaspoons cider vinegar

¼ teaspoon salt

6 large skinless chicken drumsticks (about 1½ pounds)

Adult Help Needed

1. Set the rack in the middle of the oven. Preheat oven to 375 degrees. Line a shallow baking pan with a sheet of aluminum foil.

2. Combine the ketchup, molasses, brown sugar, mustard, vinegar, and salt in a small saucepan. Bring to a boil over medium-high heat. Turn heat to low and simmer for 5 minutes.

3. Arrange the drumsticks in an even layer in the baking pan. Using a pastry brush or spoon, spread the sauce evenly on the drumsticks, turning to coat all sides.

4. Bake for 35 minutes, or until browned. Using oven mitts, remove the dish from oven and set on a cooling rack for 5 minutes. Serve hot.

Serves 3 or 4

Crusty Fish Fillets

Here's a simple way to get fish fillets dressed up with a buttery sauce.

1 cup Homemade Bread Crumbs (see page 83)

½ teaspoon salt

½ teaspoon black pepper

1 egg

4 sole fillets (about 4 ounces each)

2 tablespoons butter

1 tablespoon fresh lemon juice

**Adult
Help
Needed**

1. Set the rack in the middle of the oven. Preheat oven to 400 degrees. Line a shallow baking pan with aluminum foil.

2. In a shallow bowl crack the egg and mix with a fork. On a large plate, mix the bread crumbs, salt, and pepper. Working with 1 fillet at a time, dip each fillet in the egg mixture turning to coat each side completely. Then dip the fillet in the bread crumbs. Shake off any excess bread crumbs. Place breaded fish in baking pan.

3. Place the baking pan in oven and bake fillets for 10 minutes, or until browned. Using oven mitts, remove pan from the oven.

4. Combine butter and lemon juice in a small saucepan and cook on low until the butter is melted. Using a pot holder, remove the pan from the heat. Pour sauce over the fish and serve.

Serves 4

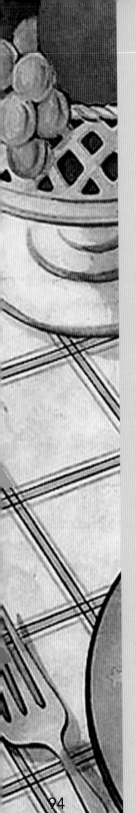

Creamy Macaroni and Cheese

If you like your mac and cheese extra creamy skip the baking in the oven step. For a crispier version, bake it.

3 tablespoons butter

2 quarts (8 cups) of cold water

½ pound uncooked elbow macaroni

1 teaspoon salt

2 tablespoons all-purpose flour

2 cups milk

1½ teaspoon Dijon-style mustard

2 cups sharp Cheddar cheese, shredded

1 cup Mozzarella cheese, shredded

Freshly ground black pepper, to taste

Adult Help Needed

1. Set the rack in the middle of the oven. Preheat oven to 350 degrees. Grease a 2-quart casserole dish with 1 tablespoon of the butter.

2. Fill a large, heavy pot halfway with 2 quarts (8 cups) of cold water. Turn heat on high and bring water to a rolling boil. Add the macaroni and salt, then cook for 10 minutes. Stir occasionally with a long wooden spoon or fork to keep pasta from sticking together. Set a colander in the sink. With adult help, use pot holders to remove pot from heat. Pour contents of the pot away from you and into a colander, and drain well.

3. In a medium saucepan, melt the remaining 2 tablespoons of butter over medium-low heat. With a whisk, stir in the flour until smooth and bubbly. Slowly pour in the milk, in parts, whisking well each time to blend all of the flour mixture into the milk. (The mixture will start to thicken.) When all of the milk has been added, continue to whisk until you have a smooth sauce. Stir in the mustard.

4. Slowly add the cheddar and mozzarella cheese to the sauce, stirring until completely melted and thoroughly mixed. Add cooked macaroni to the sauce and stir well. Spoon into the prepared baking dish. Place the dish in the oven and bake until crusty and brown on the top, about 25 minutes. Using oven mitts, remove the dish from oven and set on a cooling rack for 5 minutes. Serve hot.

Serves 6

Add-Ins

1 tomato, sliced thinly and layered on the top of macaroni mixture and bake.

1 cup bread crumbs sprinkled on top of macaroni mixture. Dot with butter and bake.

Ohio Sloppy Joe

*This scrumptious sandwich requires a few extra napkins.
No one knows if there was ever a man named Joe behind
this recipe, but it is absolutely certain that kids love it,
especially the hungry wolves. Serve with chips and pickles.*

1 tablespoon vegetable oil

1 small onion, finely chopped

3 cloves garlic, finely chopped

1 stalk celery, finely chopped

1 green pepper, finely chopped

1¼ pounds lean ground beef

1 can (14½-ounce) crushed tomatoes

2 tablespoons brown sugar

2 tablespoons Worcestershire sauce

¼ cup ketchup

4 hamburger rolls or thick slices of toast

Adult Help Needed

1. In a large skillet, heat oil over medium-low heat. Add chopped onion, garlic, celery, and green pepper. Cook, stirring occasionally, until onion is clear, about 5 minutes. Add the beef to the skillet. Cook, breaking up the meat with a spoon, until brown, for about 10 minutes.

2. Stir the tomato sauce, brown sugar, Worcestershire sauce, and ketchup into beef mixture until well blended. Simmer until thickened, stirring occasionally, about 20 minutes. For a thinner sauce add 2 tablespoons of water while it simmers.

3. Open the hamburger rolls and place on serving plates. Spoon the Sloppy Joe mixture generously over rolls. If using toast, place 2 pieces on each plate. Serve immediately. You may need to use a knife and fork.

Serves 4

Quick Breads and Cakes

Fluffy Buttermilk Pancakes

Mom's Breakfast Coffee Cake

Sunny Day Cheese Biscuits

Blackberry Muffins

Surprise Corn Muffins

Gingerbread Cake

Banana Bread

Everyday Cupcakes

Buttercream Frosting

Strawberry Shortcake

Strawberry Topping

Hot-Milk Sponge Cake

In-a-Hurry Icing

BUTTER

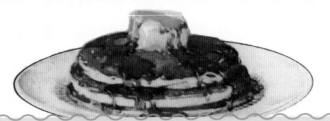

Fluffy Buttermilk Pancakes

If you don't have buttermilk on hand, stir a tablespoon of lemon juice or cider vinegar into one cup of milk and let it stand for about ten minutes before using.

1 cup all-purpose flour

2 tablespoons sugar

1 teaspoon baking powder

¼ teaspoon baking soda

½ teaspoon salt

1 cup buttermilk

1 egg

2 tablespoons vegetable oil, plus extra for greasing skillet

Adult Help Needed

1. Preheat oven to 200 degrees. In a large bowl mix the flour, sugar, baking powder, baking soda, and salt.

2. In a small bowl combine the buttermilk, egg, and 2 tablespoons oil and whisk until blended. Add the buttermilk mixture to the flour mixture, and stir just until combined. (The batter will still be a little lumpy.)

2. Pour 1 teaspoon of remaining oil in a large skillet or on a griddle. Use a paper towel to spread oil evenly across the bottom. Heat the skillet or griddle over medium-high heat. Test the heat by sprinkling a drop of water in skillet or on griddle. If it bounces away, the skillet or griddle is heated and ready to use. Using a ¼-cup measure or large spoon, pour batter into the skillet or on griddle, leaving about 1 inch between each pancake. When bubbles start to appear on top of the pancakes and the edges start to look dry, slide a spatula under each pancake and turn. Cook for about 3 more minutes, or until golden underneath.

3. Place cooked pancakes on a heatproof plate and keep warm in the oven. Cook remaining batter as directed. Serve pancakes hot with maple syrup and butter.

Makes about 8 3-inch pancakes

Toppings

For fruit pancakes, sprinkle a teaspoon of fresh blueberries, sliced strawberries, or sliced banana on each pancake just as bubbles begin to appear on the surface of the batter.

Mom's Breakfast Coffee Cake

My mom made this coffee cake for special weekend breakfasts.
The aroma in the kitchen will get the sleepy heads out of bed in a hurry.

Streusel

½ cup brown sugar, packed

¼ cup all-purpose flour

½ teaspoon ground cinnamon

3 tablespoons cold butter

Batter

½ cup (1 stick) butter, cut in half

2 cups all-purpose flour

1 cup granulated sugar

1 tablespoon baking powder

½ teaspoon salt

1 cup milk

1 egg

1. Set the rack in the middle of the oven. Preheat oven to 350 degrees. Grease an 8-inch square cake pan.

2. For the streusel: In a small bowl combine the brown sugar, ¼ cup flour, and cinnamon. Cut the 3 tablespoons of butter into small pieces and add to the bowl. Use clean fingertips to pinch butter into flour mixture until crumbly. Set aside.

3. For the batter: Put the butter pieces in a small saucepan over medium-low heat. Stir with a wooden spoon until melted. Set aside to cool. In a large bowl combine the 2 cups of flour, granulated sugar, baking powder, and salt. Stir with wooden spoon or an electric mixer until well blended. Add the melted butter, milk, and egg to the flour mixture and stir until well blended.

Adult Help Needed

4. Pour half the batter into the prepared baking pan. Sprinkle with half the streusel mixture. Pour the remaining batter on top and sprinkle with the remaining streusel mixture. Bake for 30 minutes, or until a toothpick inserted in the center comes out clean. Using oven mitts, remove the pan from the oven and place on a wire rack to cool for 5 minutes. Cut into squares and serve warm.

Serves 6 to 8

Sunny Day Cheese Biscuits

These sunny biscuits go straight from the bowl to the baking sheet so preparation and clean-up are a snap!

2 cups all-purpose flour

2 teaspoons baking powder

½ teaspoon salt

¼ cup (½ stick) cold butter, cut into small pieces

1 cup Cheddar cheese, shredded

1 cup milk

Adult Help Needed

1. Set the rack in the middle of the oven. Preheat oven to 450 degrees. Set out baking sheet. Set aside.

2. In a large bowl combine the flour, baking powder, and salt. Add the butter and cheese. Use clean fingertips to pinch butter and cheese into the flour mixture until the dough is crumbly.

3. Add the milk, stirring with a fork, just until the dough is soft.

4. Drop dough in tablespoonfuls onto greased baking sheet about 1 inch apart. Bake for 15 minutes, or until golden on the top. Using oven mitts, remove the baking sheet from the oven and place on a wire rack to cool for 3 minutes. Serve biscuits warm.

Makes 8 biscuits

Blackberry Muffins

We make our blackberry muffins in the summer using fresh blackberries, but any summer berry works well in this basic recipe. Try using a blend of strawberries, raspberries, or blueberries for extra-fruity muffins.

½ cup (1 stick) butter, cut in half

2 cups all-purpose flour

¾ cup granulated sugar

1 teaspoons baking powder

¼ teaspoon salt

1 teaspoon ground cinnamon

1 egg

1 cup milk

1½ cups fresh blackberries

Adult Help Needed

1. Set the rack in the middle of the oven. Preheat oven to 375 degrees. Generously grease 12 muffin cups or line cups with paper liners. Set aside.

2. Put the butter pieces in a small saucepan over medium-low heat. Stir with a wooden spoon until melted. Set aside to cool.

3. In a large bowl, combine the flour, sugar, baking powder, salt, and cinnamon. Whisk to mix well.

4. In a medium bowl break the egg and whisk with fork until light and foamy, then gradually stir in the milk. Add the cooled butter to the egg mixture and whisk well.

5. Pour the butter mixture into the flour mixture all at once. Stir with a wooden spoon or an electric mixer just until the batter is moistened. (The batter should look a little lumpy.) Gently stir in the blackberries.

6. Using a small measuring cup or a spoon, fill the muffin cups about two-thirds full of batter. Bake for 20 minutes, or until a toothpick inserted in the center comes out clean. Using oven mitts, remove the pan from the oven and place on a wire rack to cool for 5 minutes. To help loosen the muffins from the pan, run a butter knife along the inside edges of the muffin cups. Serve warm.

Makes 1 dozen muffins

Surprise Corn Muffins

If you place jam in the middle of each muffin before baking, you'll have a warm fruity center to enjoy. Left over corn muffins are delicious when split and toasted or grilled.

½ cup (1 stick) butter, cut in half

1½ cups all-purpose flour

2 tablespoons sugar

2¼ teaspoons baking powder

¾ teaspoon salt

¾ cup yellow cornmeal

2 eggs

1 cup milk

½ cup raspberry (or other favorite flavor) jam

Adult Help Needed

1. Set the rack in the middle of the oven. Preheat oven to 425 degrees. Generously grease 12 muffin cups or line cups with paper liners. Set aside.

2. Put the butter pieces in a small saucepan over medium-low heat. Stir with a wooden spoon until melted. Set aside to cool.

3. In a large bowl combine the flour, sugar, baking powder, and salt. Add the cornmeal and mix well.

4. In a small bowl whisk together the eggs and milk. Add the cooled butter to the egg mixture and whisk well. Pour the mixture all at once into flour, stirring just until batter is moistened. (The batter should look a little lumpy.)

5. Using a small measuring cup or a spoon, fill each muffin cup about one-third full with batter. Drop 2 teaspoonfuls of jam on each muffin, then cover the jam with another layer of batter, filling each cup about two-thirds full. Bake for 20 minutes, or until a toothpick inserted in the center comes out clean. Using oven mitts, remove the pan from the oven and place on a wire rack to cool for 5 minutes. To help loosen the muffins from the pan, run a butter knife along the inside edges of the muffin cup. Serve warm.

Makes 1 dozen muffins

Gingerbread Cake

My grandmother's gingerbread is more like a cake than bread. For an old-fashioned finishing touch, sprinkle confectioners' sugar on top. This cake gets even more flavorful on the second day.

2 cups all-purpose flour

2 teaspoons baking powder

2 teaspoons ground ginger

1 teaspoon ground cinnamon

¼ teaspoon ground cloves

½ teaspoon salt

¼ teaspoon baking soda

6 tablespoons (½ stick) butter, softened

2 tablespoon vegetable oil

½ cup sugar

1 egg

¾ cup molasses

¾ cup buttermilk (see page 100)

1 tablespoon confectioners' sugar (optional)

1. Set the rack in the middle of the oven. Preheat oven to 350 degrees. Grease an 8-inch square baking pan. Set aside.

2. In a medium bowl combine the flour, baking powder, ginger, cinnamon, cloves, salt, and baking soda. Mix well to combine.

3. In a large bowl, using a wooden spoon or an electric mixer, beat the butter and oil until creamy. Add the sugar a little at a time, mixing until light and fluffy. Beat in the egg and molasses. (Don't worry if the batter looks curdled.) Add about one-third of the flour mixture and stir to combine. Stir in about half the buttermilk. Beat until smooth. The color of the batter will be a dark golden color. Stir in half the remaining flour, then add all the remaining buttermilk. Stir in the remaining flour and mix until the batter is smooth.

4. Pour the batter into the prepared pan. Bake for 45 minutes, or until a toothpick inserted in the center comes out clean. Using oven mitts, remove the pan from the oven and place on a wire rack to cool for 10 minutes. Using a small strainer, dust confectioners' sugar over the top. Cut gingerbread into squares and serve warm.

Makes 9 to 12 squares

Banana Bread

If you have slightly overripe bananas in the kitchen, don't throw them away. Use them to make this sweet and tasty cake.

1¾ cups all-purpose flour

2 teaspoons baking powder

½ teaspoon salt

¼ teaspoon baking soda

½ cup (1 stick) butter, at room temperature

½ cup sugar

2 large eggs

1 cup mashed bananas (about 3)

1. Set the rack in the middle of the oven. Preheat oven to 350 degrees. Grease an 8½- by 4½-inch loaf pan or an 8-inch square baking pan. Set aside.

2. In a large bowl, combine the flour, baking powder, salt, and baking soda. In a separate bowl, using a wooden spoon or an electric mixer, beat the butter and sugar until light and fluffy. Add the eggs and beat well. Stir in the mashed bananas, then gradually add flour mixture, in parts, until the ingredients are well blended. The batter will be slightly stiff.

3. Use a rubber spatula to scrape the batter into the greased pan. Bake for 60 minutes, or until golden brown on top. Using oven mitts, remove the pan from the oven and place on a wire rack to cool for 15 minutes. Cut into thick slices or squares and serve warm.

Serves 6 to 8

Everyday Cupcakes

Cupcakes are delightful to eat and special to have any time. Make a batch for special events at school or just to have around the house for dessert.

½ cup (1 stick) butter, softened

1 cup sugar

3 eggs

1 teaspoon vanilla extract

2 cups all-purpose flour

2 teaspoons baking powder

¼ teaspoon salt

¾ cup milk

Adult Help Needed

1. Set the rack in the middle of the oven. Preheat oven to 375 degrees. Line 24 muffins cups with paper liners. Set aside.

2. In a large bowl, using a wooden spoon or an electric mixer, beat the butter and sugar until light and fluffy. Add the egg and vanilla and beat until smooth. In a small bowl whisk together flour, baking powder, and salt.

3. Add half the flour mixture to butter mixture and beat until combined. Slowly add the milk until mixed. Beat in the remaining flour until the batter is smooth.

4. Using a large spoon or small measuring cup, fill each muffin cup half full. Bake for 20 minutes, or until a toothpick inserted in the center comes out clean. Using oven mitts, remove the pan from the oven and place on a wire rack and cool completely. Remove cupcakes from the pan and frost with Buttercream Frosting (recipe below).

Makes 2 dozen cupcakes

Buttercream Frosting

1½ cups confectioners' sugar

½ cup (1 stick) unsalted butter, softened

1 tablespoon milk

1 teaspoon vanilla extract

In a large bowl, using a wooden spoon or an electric mixer, beat together confectioners' sugar, butter, milk, and vanilla until smooth. If necessary add more milk until frosting is spreading consistency. Spread over cooled cupcakes with a butter knife or rubber spatula.

Makes enough to frost 2 dozen cupcakes

Strawberry Shortcake

For special summer suppers my grandmother would bake shortcakes and serve them warm with freshly picked, lightly sugared strawberries. We feasted until we had our fill.

2 cups all-purpose flour

3 tablespoons sugar

1 tablespoon baking powder

½ teaspoon salt

½ cup (1 stick) cold butter, plus soft butter for serving

¾ cup milk

Strawberry Topping (see page 117)

Adult Help Needed

1. Set the rack in the middle of the oven. Preheat oven to 400 degrees. Grease a baking sheet. Set aside.

2. In a large bowl, combine the flour, sugar, baking powder, and salt. Mix well with a wooden spoon. Cut the butter into small pieces and add to the flour mixture. Using clean fingertips, pinch butter into the flour mixture until it is coarse and crumbly.

3. With a fork stir in the milk just until mixed. Using clean hands or a spoon, form the biscuits into 3-inch balls and place on the prepared baking sheet, about 1 inch apart.

4. Bake for 12 minutes, or until the biscuits are golden brown. Using oven mitts, remove the pan from the oven and place on a wire rack. Let biscuits cool on the baking sheet.

5. To assemble, split warm biscuits in half with a bread knife and spread with soft butter. For each serving, place 2 biscuit halves in a small bowl and top with a large spoonful of Strawberry Topping. Pour a little milk over the biscuit or top with a spoonful of Whipped Cream (see page 139).

Makes 6 shortcakes

Strawberry Topping

Make this sauce as a topping for shortcake, or just serve it by itself as a simple dessert. Peaches and nectarines are also very good when served this way.

2 pints fresh strawberries

2 tablespoons sugar

Adult Help Needed

Rinse the strawberries under cold water and drain well in a colander. Use a paring knife to remove the green caps. Cut berries into quarters placing them in a bowl as you go. Sprinkle with sugar and cover bowl. Let the berries stand at room temperature for about 30 minutes. (This helps to soften the berries and bring out their juices.)

Hot-Milk Sponge Cake

*Beating the eggs for 10 minutes gives this cake a fluffy lightness.
This cake can be eaten plain or frosted with a In-a-Hurry-Icing
(recipe follows), or topped with seasonal fruit or canned peaches.*

½ cup milk

1 cup all-purpose flour

1 teaspoon baking powder

3 eggs

1 cup sugar

1 teaspoon vanilla extract

**Adult
Help
Needed**

1. Set the rack in the middle of the oven. Preheat oven to 350 degrees. Grease a 8-inch square baking pan. Set aside.

2. In a small saucepan warm the milk over medium-low heat until it almost boils. Turn off heat and cover the pan with a lid to keep warm.

3. In a large bowl combine the flour, baking powder, and salt. In a separate bowl, using an electric mixer, beat the eggs until very thick and light in color, about 12 minutes. Slowly add the sugar, about ¼ cup at a time, and continue to beat until the sugar is well blended. Add the vanilla and beat for 2 more minutes.

4. Using a rubber spatula, carefully add the flour mixture in parts, mixing gently until all the flour has been added and is well blended.

5. Add the warm milk to batter. Mix just until the batter is smooth and light. Pour batter into the prepared pan. Bake for 35 minutes or until a toothpick inserted in the center comes out clean. Using oven mitts, remove the pan from the oven and place on a wire rack to cool completely. When cool, glaze with In-a-Hurry Icing or sprinkle with confectioners' sugar.

In-a-Hurry Icing

When you need a quick icing for any cake, try this recipe.

6 tablespoons apricot jam

2 teaspoons water

Place jam in a small saucepan and heat over medium-low heat, stirring, until jam is melted. Add water and stir well. Use a pot holder to remove the pan from the heat. Use a pastry brush or a rubber spatula to smooth jam on top of cake.

Cookies and Simple Desserts

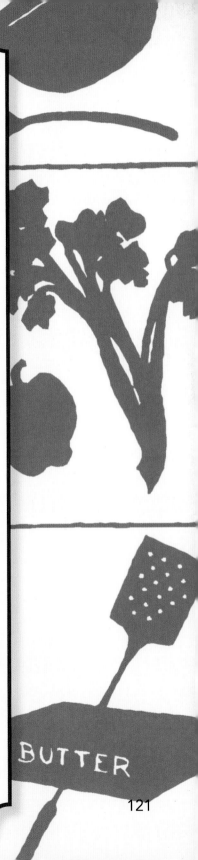

Icebox Cookies

Snickerdoodles

Peanut Butter Cookies

Heirloom Brownies

Lemon Bars

Spicy Applesauce

Baked Apples

Minta's Apple Crisp

Baked Bananas

Chocolate-Dipped Fruit

Rainy Day Rice Pudding

Best Chocolate Pudding

Jackie's Lemon Jelly

Whipped Cream

Whipped Cream Dream

121

Icebox Cookies

With icebox cookies you can have freshly baked cookies anytime.
Store the rolled dough in the refrigerator, then slice and bake
cookies whenever you want them.

½ cup (1 stick), butter softened

½ cup white granulated sugar

½ cup brown sugar

1 teaspoon vanilla extract

2 eggs

2¾ cups all purpose flour

½ teaspoon baking soda

½ teaspoon salt

Adult Help Needed

1. In a large bowl combine the butter, granulated and brown sugars, and vanilla. Using a wooden spoon or an electric mixer, beat the ingredients until smooth. Add the eggs and combine well.

2. In a separate bowl combine the flour, baking soda, and salt. Whisk to mix well. Add to butter mixture and stir until well blended. Divide the dough in half and place each on a sheet of waxed paper. Use your hands to form each half of dough into a roll about 2 inches across. Wrap each roll in waxed paper and chill for at least 2 hours, or overnight.

Baking Icebox Cookies

Adult Help Needed

1. Set the rack in the middle of the oven. Preheat oven to 375 degrees. Lightly grease a baking sheet. Carefully slice the log in as many ½-inch thick rounds as you need. Place on baking sheet, leaving 1 inch between each round. Bake for 8 to 10 minutes, or until golden.

2. Using oven mitts, remove the baking sheet from the oven and place on a wire rack to cool for 3 minutes. Use a spatula to transfer warm cookies to the rack and cool completely.

Add-Ins

Mix in one of these items to dough before shaping into a log:

½ cup chocolate chips

½ cup dried cranberries or raisins

½ cup almonds, chopped fine

Snickerdoodles

As kids, my sisters and I made these cookies when we were just hanging around. Nowadays, kids are really busy, but maybe you can find a good reason to hang around and make Snickerdoodles with your friends. These cookies are delicious when they are a little soft so don't overbake.

1 cup (2 sticks) butter, softened

1½ cups sugar, plus 3 tablespoons

2 eggs

2 cups all-purpose flour

2 teaspoons cream of tartar

1 teaspoon baking soda

¼ teaspoon salt

1 tablespoon ground cinnamon

Adult Help Needed

1. Set the rack in the middle of the oven. Preheat oven to 350 degrees. Lightly grease 2 baking sheets. Set aside.

2. In a large bowl using a wooden spoon or an electric mixer, cream the butter and the 1½ cups sugar until fluffy. Add the eggs, one at a time, beating until smooth after each addition.

3. In a separate bowl combine the flour, cream of tartar, baking soda, and salt. Whisk to mix well. Gradually add flour mixture to the butter mixture. Stir until the dough is smooth. Cover the bowl and chill in the refrigerator for 10 minutes.

4. Combine the remaining 3 tablespoons of sugar and the cinnamon in a small bowl.

5. Remove the cookie dough from refrigerator. Using clean hands or a spoon, shape dough into 1-inch balls. Roll the balls, one at a time, in the sugar and cinnamon mixture until well coated, then place on a prepared baking sheet about 2 inches apart. Bake the cookies for 10 minutes, or until lightly golden.

6. Using oven mitts, remove the baking sheet from the oven and place on a wire rack to cool for 3 minutes. Use a spatula to transfer warm cookies to the rack and cool a few minutes. Continue rolling and baking dough as directed, regreasing baking sheets if necessary. Serve warm with a glass of cold milk.

Makes 4 dozen cookies

Peanut Butter Cookies

The sign of a real peanut butter cookie is the criss-cross pattern on top that you make with a fork. For variety press your thumb gently in the center of each cookie then fill thumbprint with your favorite jam or jelly or a chocolate chip after baking.

1 cup natural peanut butter

½ cup (1 stick) butter, softened

½ cup granulated sugar

½ cup firmly packed light brown sugar

1 egg

1 teaspoon vanilla extract

2½ cups all-purpose flour

1 teaspoon baking soda

¼ teaspoon salt

1. Set the rack in the middle of the oven. Preheat oven to 375 degrees. Lightly grease 2 baking sheets. Set aside.

2. In a large bowl, using wooden spoon or an electric mixer, cream the peanut butter and butter, then beat in the granulated and brown sugars until creamy. Add the egg and vanilla and mix until smooth.

3. In a separate bowl add the flour, baking soda, and salt. Whisk to mix well. Gradually stir into the peanut butter mixture until thoroughly mixed.

4. Using clean hands or a spoon, shape dough into 1-inch balls. Place balls on one of the baking sheets about 2 inches apart. Repeat until the baking sheet is full. Flatten each ball using a fork dipped in flour. Make a criss-cross pattern by pressing the fork in one direction and then crossing over in the opposite direction. Bake for 10 minutes, or until golden.

5. Using oven mitts, remove the baking sheet from the oven and place on a wire rack to cool for 3 minutes. Use a spatula to transfer warm cookies to the rack and cool completely. Continue rolling and baking dough as directed, regreasing baking sheets if necessary.

Makes 3 dozen cookies

Heirloom Brownies

This is a brownie lover's brownie. It is crusty on the top, soft in the middle, and rich throughout. Make an extra batch to share with friends.

5 tablespoons butter

2 squares (1 ounce each) unsweetened chocolate

1 cup sugar

2 eggs, lightly beaten

1 teaspoon vanilla extract

¾ cup all-purpose flour

½ teaspoon baking powder

½ teaspoon salt

Adult Help Needed

1. Set the rack in the middle of the oven. Preheat oven to 350 degrees. Grease an 8-inch square baking pan. Set aside.

2. In a small saucepan, combine the butter and chocolate. Melt over low heat, stirring occasionally with a wooden spoon, until the butter and chocolate are completely smooth.

3. Using a pot holder, remove the pan from the heat. With a rubber spatula, scrape the chocolate mixture into a large bowl. Stir in the sugar, eggs, and vanilla and mix until smooth. Add the flour, baking powder, and salt and combine well. Pour the batter into the prepared pan.

4. Bake for 25 minutes, or until a toothpick inserted in the center comes out clean. Using oven mitts, remove the pan from the oven and place on a wire rack to cool for 5 minutes. Cut into squares.

Makes 16 brownies

Lemon Bars

This dessert is sweet, tart, and buttery all at once. Organic lemons are best for zesting. If you can't find organic, be sure to wash the lemon very well to remove any pesticides or wax.

1 cup all-purpose flour

½ cup confectioners' sugar, plus more for dusting

Pinch of salt (for crust)

4 ounces (1 stick) unsalted butter, softened

2 large eggs

1 cup granulated sugar

2 tablespoon all-purpose flour

Pinch of salt (for filling)

¼ cup freshly squeezed lemon juice

2 teaspoons finely grated lemon zest

Adult Help Needed

1. Set the rack in the middle of the oven. Preheat oven to 350 degrees. Grease an 8-inch square baking pan.

2. *For the crust:* Combine the flour, confectioners' sugar, and salt in the bowl. Add butter and with clean fingertips, pinch butter into flour mixture together until crumbly. Press the mixture evenly into the bottom of your prepared pan. Bake about 15 minutes or until golden. Using oven mitts, remove the pan from the oven and place on a wire rack to cool.

3. *To make the filling:* In a medium bowl whisk together eggs, sugar, flour, and salt. Whisk in lemon juice and lemon zest until well combined. Pour lemon mixture over the crust (it's okay if crust is still hot). Bake until filling is just set, about 20 minutes. Using oven mitts, remove the pan from the oven and place on a wire rack to cool completely before cutting into squares. Dust with confectioners' sugar if desired.

Make 20 2-inch squares

Spicy Applesauce

Fresh applesauce can be eaten at any meal. If you use sweet apples, you may not want to add any sugar.

6 large apples, such as Golden Delicious, Macintosh, or Jonagold

2 tablespoons sugar

¼ cup water

½ teaspoon ground cinnamon, or more to taste

Adult Help Needed

1. Cut apples into quarters. Use a paring knife to cut off the peels, and remove the cores.

2. Put apples, sugar, and water in medium saucepan and turn heat on medium-low and simmer 15 minutes or until apples are soft. Stir frequently. Mash the cooked apples to a texture you like.

3. Using a pot holder, remove the pan from the heat and allow sauce to cool. Stir in cinnamon and mix well. Serve warm or cold in small dessert bowls.

Makes 2 cups

Baked Apples

Simple and satisfying, this old-fashioned dessert is bound to become a family favorite. The baked apples also make a nice dish for a wintertime breakfast.

4 large red apples

4 teaspoons sugar

4 teaspoons salted butter, softened

1 teaspoon ground cinnamon

2 tablespoons water

Adult Help Needed

1. Set the rack in the middle of the oven. Preheat oven to 350 degrees. Wash apples and core. (To core an apple, use a paring knife to cut out the stem area and then the core, or the middle, of the apple.)

2. In the hollow of each apple, place 1 teaspoon sugar, 1 teaspoon butter, and ¼ teaspoon ground cinnamon.

3. Set apples upright in a baking dish. Pour the water in bottom of the dish and cover with a lid or aluminum foil. Bake for 30 minutes, or until the apple is soft. Using oven mitts, remove the dish from the oven. Let the apples cool for a few minutes.

4. Serve each apple in a small bowl, topped with milk or cream.

Serves 4

Minta's Apple Crisp

*Cooking apples such as Braeburn, Cortland, and Golden Delicious,
work well for this dish, but you can use whatever is on hand.
Serve in small dessert bowls and pour a little milk or cream over the crisp.*

8 large cooking apples

½ teaspoon ground cinnamon

½ cup sugar

¼ cup water or apple cider

¾ cup all-purpose flour

½ cup (1 stick) butter, cut into pieces

**Adult
Help
Needed**

1. Set the rack in the middle of the oven. Preheat oven to 350 degrees.
Butter 8-inch square baking pan.

2. Cut apples into quarters. Use a paring knife to cut off the peels,
and remove the cores. Cut quarters into 3 thin slices each and spread
on the bottom of the baking dish. Sprinkle apples with the cinnamon
and 2 tablespoons of sugar. Stir apples to coat evenly with the mixture.
Add the ¼ cup water or cider to the bottom of the pan.

3. In a medium bowl combine the remaining sugar, flour, and butter.
With clean fingertips, pinch butter into flour mixture together until
crumbly. Sprinkle the mixture over the apples. Bake for 30 minutes,
or until golden brown. Using oven mitts, remove the pan from the oven.
Let cool for a few minutes. Spoon into bowls and serve warm.

Serves 6 to 8

Baked Bananas

Baking bananas in butter and brown sugar makes a luscious dessert.

4 firm, ripe bananas

¼ cup brown sugar

3 tablespoons butter, cut in smaller pieces

2 tablespoon water

1 tablespoon fresh lemon juice

Adult Help Needed

1. Set the rack in the middle of the oven. Preheat oven to 350 degrees. Grease an 8-inch square baking pan. Set aside.

2. Peel bananas and slice in half lengthwise. Place halves in a baking dish. Sprinkle the brown sugar over the bananas and dot with butter. Add the water and lemon juice to the bottom of the pan. Bake for 20 minutes. Using oven mitts, remove the pan from the oven. Serve warm, with or without vanilla ice cream.

Serves 4

Chocolate-Dipped Fruit

Try dipping fresh fruit into a bowl of warm Chocolate Sauce (see page 23). Use whole strawberries, whole cherries, sliced apples, peaches, pears, banana, and fresh pineapple chunks. Let the dipped fruit cool on a foiled lined baking sheet or eat right away!

Rainy Day Rice Pudding

One of the best things about this rice pudding is that you mix and bake everything in one dish. Make it on a rainy day when you know will be inside.

1 cup uncooked long-grain rice

1 quart whole milk

½ cup sugar

2 teaspoons vanilla extract

½ teaspoon salt

Pinch of ground nutmeg or cinnamon

Adult Help Needed

1. Set the rack in the middle of the oven. Preheat oven to 300 degrees. Butter a 1½-quart baking dish.

2. Combine the rice, milk, sugar, salt, vanilla, and nutmeg in the baking dish. Stir well. Place in the center of the oven and bake uncovered for 1½ hours.

3. Using oven mitts, remove the dish from the oven to cool. Serve the pudding warm, sprinkled with a pinch of ground nutmeg or cinnamon before serving.

Serves 6

Best Chocolate Pudding

This pudding makes a rich, smooth, and chocolaty dessert. It's loaded with calcium so it's also a good choice for a special snack. Using a double boiler pan makes a smoother pudding but you can also make this in a saucepan.

1 cup water, for boiling

¼ cup cornstarch

½ cup sugar

Pinch of salt

3 cups milk

4 tablespoons unsweetened cocoa powder

1 teaspoon vanilla extract

Adult Help Needed

1. Add 1 cup of water to the bottom pan of a double boiler. Place the cornstarch, sugar, and salt in the top pan of a double boiler.

2. Over a medium-high heat, slowly add the milk, chocolate, and vanilla to the cornstarch mixture, stirring constantly with a wooden spoon, until the mixture is thick and smooth, about 5 minutes. As pudding thickens, scrape sides with the wooden spoon and stir back into the mixture until smooth. Cook for 2 more minutes, stirring occasionally.

3. Pour pudding into 6 serving cups. Refrigerate until chilled.

Makes 6 ½-cup servings

Jackie's Lemon Jelly

This is a do-it-yourself gelatin dessert. Add fresh fruit to make it light and refreshing or serve plain topped with Whipped Cream (see page 139).

1½ cup water

1 envelope (1 tablespoon) gelatin

½ cup sugar

½ cup fresh lemon juice

1 cup fresh blueberries, seedless grapes, or sliced bananas

Adult Help Needed

1. Set out a heatproof serving bowl. Squeeze lemons for juice and set aside. Wash fruit and let it drain in colander.

2. Put the water in a medium saucepan and bring to a boil over high heat. Turn down the heat to medium-high and add sugar, stirring to dissolve. Sprinkle in the gelatin and stir well. The liquid will begin to thicken in a few minutes. Turn off the heat and add the lemon juice.

3. Using a pot holder, pour mixture into serving bowl. Add 1 cup fresh blueberries, seedless grapes, or sliced bananas to the warm gelatin mixture. Cover and chill in refrigerator until firm, for about 1 hour.

Serves 6

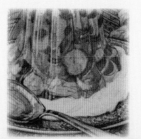

Whipped Cream

1 cup chilled heavy or whipping cream

¼ cup confectioners' sugar

Pour the cream in a medium bowl and beat with a rotary beater or a whisk until soft peaks form. Add confectioners' sugar and fold gently into whipped cream. Use right away or chill in refrigerator until ready to use. It will keep for up to 2 hours.

Whipped Cream Dream

Here's a dreamy dessert that will have all of the kids talking for days. Layer fresh berries and whipped cream in parfait glasses and a garnish with mint leaves.

1. Wash 1 cup each of fresh raspberries and strawberries in a colander and drain.

2. In 4 small bowls or parfait glasses, add berries to the bottom of the cup then spoon a thick dollop of whipped cream, then add layer of berries. Top off with another dollop of whipped cream and garnish with few more berries, a mint leaf, or a cherry. Serve chilled.

Serves 6

Favorite Recipes

Favorite Recipes

Favorite Recipes

Index